one moment that being a grandmother must mean that you are now definitely old, ineffective and generally past it. You may be a decade younger, but the average age for entering the grandparent stakes is fifty for a woman, fifty-two for a man. This is the age at which competence and experience combine to produce peak performance in whatever you set your mind to.

As well as being a grandmother, you may be a dynamic business executive, a Prime Minister or the Queen, an actress like Brigitte Bardot – or the unassuming force that holds a family together and enables each member to fulfil his or her potential. I have been a grandmother for some years now and my grand-children cover a wide age span. The eldest is a teenager, the youngest is just learning to walk. I'm not an old-style stereotype granny with nothing more in my life but to sit by the fireside knitting tiny garments. I have my work as a consultant psychia-trist, with a special interest in family relationships, and my own pleasures: writing, nature, antiques and, of course, TV.

My role as a grandparent is different from anything else I've ever done. What I learned bringing up my own children doesn't apply: steam radio in an age of television. Besides, the relationship between grandchild and grandmother is special and unique and can have a profound influence. I am not forgetting grandfathers. They are loved and respected by their grandchildren and may see no necessity to delve into their responsibilities by reading about them. Grandmothers, by contrast, are often aware of the complex-ity and importance of their position: which is why we need to share all we know. The grandmother is the first reserve in the case of family illness, heartbreak or financial disaster – often with a hands-on role.

DEMOGRAPHY AND STATISTICS

Depending on your age when your children were born and their ages when they have their babies, you may qualify as a grand-mother from around forty onwards. On average you are likely to hold this new, engrossing job for upwards of a third of your life. We belong to an increasingly large section of society. At the beginning of the 1990s, there were 8.8 million people of sixty-five plus in the UK, well into the grandparent range. The number is predicted to rise to 11.4 million by 2025. This gives us enormous political clout if we should ever decide to use it, but our main influence is personal.

The remit of a grandmother encompasses more than ever before. It extends from nappy-changer to provider of treats, peace-maker, knowledgeable careers adviser, and sensitive therapist to a youngster in emotional turmoil. Jack Nicholson and Marlon Brando are just two of an army of successful people who were brought up by their grandmothers, while it is to his granny that Desmond Morris owes his lifelong affair with nature. She provided him with an escape from the city into the wilds of the countryside.

Modern families

Today's grandmothers have to be flexible, to cope with many different types of family in our fascinating, confusing multicultural society. The old stereotype of a father going out to work, married to a mother at home with 2.4 children, all mildly C of E, is now the exception. Even in the most conventional families, the majority of mothers have a job outside the home, for the sake of the money, apart from interest. It is increasingly common for mothers to delay having children until they are well into their thirties or even their early forties. This can put you in the strange situation of having friends of your generation with young children who are not much older than your grandchild.

One in three marriages today ends in divorce and the prevalence of single motherhood has hit an all-time high. Partnerships without the ritual and trappings of a wedding ceremony are increasingly popular, and no less likely to be stable than a marriage. Throughout this book, the terms husband and wife and partner are seen as interchangeable and daughter-in-law and son-in-law refer to your children's partners, whether they are married or not. My daughter and her long-term partner married a few months ago – because their children said they would prefer that arrangement. Nothing else has changed.

The different cultures and family traditions that enrich our

You and
Your
Grandchild

—

Dr Joan Gomez

BLOOMSBURY

Acknowledgements

I have had a lot of help – and fun – with writing this book and I am particularly grateful to Liz Moss of Croydon Libraries, Julia Heffernan of Dillons Bookstore and Peter Skinner of Hamleys Toyshop.

First published 1996 by Bloomsbury Publishing Plc, 2 Soho Square, London W1V 6HB

Copyright © 1996 Joan Gomez

The moral right of the author has been asserted

A copy of the CIP entry for this book is available from the British Library

ISBN 0 7475 2194 8

10 9 8 7 6 5 4 3 2 1

Designed by Hugh Adams, AB3
Typeset by Hewer Text Composition Services, Edinburgh
Printed by Cox & Wyman Ltd, Reading, Berkshire

You and Your Grandchild

Contents

Introduction

WELCOME! Like me, you are a member, or about to be, of this huge, important club: the grandmothers. Neither money, passing exams, nor influential contacts can get you in. Instead, you must have been through a long and testing apprenticeship: as a daughter, a mother and a granddaughter, too.

I remember my 'Granny-in-New-Zealand'. She meant pictures of Maori warriors and hot springs and tiny, neat writing. She sent me embroidery sets and a prayer book, with which I married and buried my dolls. My mother's mother, Gran, was a woman of strong views and great warmth. She had a little yapping Pom – you don't see this breed nowadays – and a passion for card games. When my mother had pneumonia and nearly died, Gran came up from the country with woolly vests and farm eggs and arrowroot. My mother slowly recovered and I learned to play whist during Gran's stay. I suppose it would be bingo now.

Then there was my mother. We would call her a lone parent today. She was a part of my life: an unfailing support and a constant irritation. We hardly ever saw eye to eye during my childhood, but she made a wonderful grandmother to my brood of four natural and six equally dear adopted children. She was generous, wise and helpful when she was needed and got on with her own life at other times. The sharp edge of criticism that I had experienced from her as a child had softened and mellowed. Nothing put her out. I only wish that I could be half as good as she was at this difficult, delightful job.

How do you see it?

The terms 'granny', 'grandmother' and 'grandma' may fill your heart with a warm glow – or quite the reverse. Whichever way it strikes you, you are not alone and not abnormal. Val Hennessy and Liz Hodgkinson, writing in the *Daily Mail* on Friday, January 13th, 1994, took violently opposing views in reaction to the imminent prospect of 'becoming a granny'.

Val, who had bumped into Ruth Rendell in Selfridges, buying presents for her grandchildren, was desperate for her turn to come. She envisaged extraordinarily strong, healthy youngsters, who had by-passed the baby stage of nappies, crying and sticky fingers, and loved to go round the toyshops with her. Presumably they never screamed for the £1500 computerized train set. Other treats in store: 'they'll be allowed to stuff themselves with popcorn, crisps, cola and ice-cream . . . candyfloss and Knickerbocker Glories'; and she will take them to Longleat, Alton Towers, Majorca – and surely Disneyworld?

She may read to them from *Winnie the Pooh*, while the child on her lap will be 'gorgeous, contented, thumb-sucking'. She herself will have magenta highlights in her hair and silver biker boots – she'll be 'groovy'. No prizes for guessing where this dream will go wrong.

Liz Hodgkinson, by contrast, says flatly that she would 'absolutely hate' to be a grandmother. She resents the thought of being made into one, willy-nilly, but there isn't an opt-out clause. She is planning to take up travelling in a big way when the worst happens and to make sure that she doesn't have a spare room. She is even considering a live-in lover who hates children. Her own grandparents and her mother in turn were all first-class at the job, she admits. Her desperate, defiant plan is 90 per cent certain to come unstuck when she first meets her grandchild. It is the newborn baby's very helplessness and vulnerability that trap our emotions, doubly so if your own flesh and blood are involved.

My friend Pamela expressed a common attitude, these days. She looked worried: 'I'd like to be a good grandmother, but I don't feel like a granny at all. After all, I'm only forty-two.' Don't imagine for country add to the complexities of the task of being a grandmother. In a big, straggling Russian family spanning three generations, transplanted to Manchester after the war, it is Elena, the grandmother, who reminds her sons and daughters and teaches her grandchildren about their roots and their romantic heritage. She gives them all a sense of family and self-worth, no matter that money is sometimes tight and fashionable possessions in short supply.

THE LAW

There are important legal aspects to being a grandparent, as well as the cosiness and fun. The Children Act 1989 represents 'the most comprehensive reform of child law to come before Parliament in living memory,' said the Lord Chancellor. The legal position of grandparents was discussed at length during the debates leading up to the Act, but they are nowhere mentioned specifically except as 'relevant other persons'.

The nub of the Act is parental responsibility, which is down to each parent if the child is legitimate, or the mother only, if not. This is automatic but other people can take on parental responsibility in certain circumstances. This is where grandparents come in, as the likeliest other people to be involved. There are three ways in which a grandparent (or two grandparents) can become legally responsible for a child:

1. By obtaining a residence order
2. By becoming the child's guardian
3. By adopting the child

Residence Orders

These are awarded by the Court. Much the same as the former 'care and control' orders, they settle who the child should live with. This could be either or both grandparents.

> Enid and Jack obtained a residence order when their two-year-old grandson was tragically orphaned. His parents were both killed in a motorway pile-up. The other grandparents would have liked to take over young Andy now they had lost their son,

but they had seen very little of him up till now, living as they did near Dundee. Enid on the other hand lived only ten minutes away and had often acted as a baby-sitter. The Court decided that she and Jack were the more suitable from Andy's point of view.

It meant a major upheaval, suddenly having to cope with a two-year-old twenty-four hours a day. Enid was fifty-two and fit. She decided to continue with her part-time job – for her 'sanity's sake' – which involved getting help for the hours she wasn't around.

Contact Orders

These are another new feature which came in under the Children Act. They replace the old 'access' orders, the cause of such wrangling between the parents after a divorce. A contact order requires the person with whom the child is living to allow him or her to visit or stay with a named individual, or have some other form of contact, such as telephoning and letters.

When there are problems and misunderstandings in a family, of course the ideal solution is compromise and agreement. Nevertheless, feelings can run high and it is as well to know where you stand legally. An all too common situation arises in the wake of a divorce. The child usually lives with the mother. She may feel so bitter towards her ex and his family that she cuts off all contact with the grandparents. It doesn't have to be a divorce for this to happen. A separation when an established non-marital partnership breaks up, can lead to family schism. One parent may die and the survivor may not want to have anything to do with her, or his, in-laws.

Sheila felt it was unfair. It was not her fault that she was a mother-in-law. The marriage hadn't stood a chance from the beginning. Rory, her son, had been seven years younger than Binkie. She was thirty-five when they got married and although she looked about twenty-four, she was aware of the relentless ticking of her biological clock. After the baby was born, ten months later, Binkie lost all interest in her husband. She was 100 per cent mother. Rory put up with it for a while. Truth to tell, he had never wanted to be a father and when Binkie switched off on sex, he began to look elsewhere.

The divorce, which was ground out three years later, might have been amicable if it hadn't been for the money. Rory felt that he had been taken for a ride, while Binkie resented having to economize on the allowance the solicitors had agreed with the Court. Binkie's sense of grievance extended to Rory's parents. She would not let Rory or Sheila and Bob have so much as a sight of baby Abigail. The baby was the one who lost out: cut off from her father and deprived of the natural resources of two ordinary, loving grandparents. When Rory started proceedings for a contact order, Sheila and her husband joined in and applied for similar orders for themselves.

It wasn't the pleasantest way to achieve some involvement, but it turned out to be a blessing – to young Abigail. When she was seven her mother married a much older man. His own children were grown up and had long since left home and he found a lively chatterbox an intolerable irritation. Sheila's and Bob's house became a haven for Abigail and even Binkie was glad to dump her daughter when she and Alastair wanted a sophisticated break in Paris or Venice or Acapulco.

The other grandparents were already in their eighties, with one of them an invalid, so they could not cope with a young child for more than an hour or so. As for Abigail, visits to Granny and Granpy were her greatest security when both her parents had remarried. Rory's new wife tried to love Abigail but she could not suppress the tinge of jealousy that second wives so often feel towards their husbands' children.

If a child has lived with his or her grandparents on and off for three years or more, on an informal basis, they are entitled to apply for a residence order. This may be necessary when a parent who had handed over the care of her or his child previously, now wants to take over again. In some circumstances the youngster would be happier staying with his or her grandparents.

Alec, for example, hated his mother's new man-friend and the feeling was mutual. His mother wanted Alec to live with her and struggled to keep the peace. Then she fell pregnant and she and the boyfriend became increasingly absorbed with the new baby, whom they could truly share. Alec had stayed with his grandparents for longer and longer periods at shorter and shorter intervals, although his mother still wanted to retain control. Alec himself, now twelve, made it quite clear what he wanted, and the Court awarded a residence order to his grandparents. It makes the process easier, in fact a matter of course, if both parents, or in this case the mother, give their consent.

Sometimes – fortunately not often – there is a major family rift between the parents and grandparents, with the effect that the child never sees the latter pair. Grandparents can apply for a contact order in these circumstances, but there is no guarantee that it will be granted.

Maisie and John went through a nerve-racking time with their daughter. Lynne was a promising student with everything ahead of her when she met Jake. He was a flamboyant character, well known in the music scene and dabbling with crack and 'E'. He had been divorced twice and his three children lived with their mothers. Maisie and her husband felt they could have gone mad when Lynne threw up university and moved in with Jake. Maisie cried and John forbade Jake the house. Lynne, of course, was always welcome; but she didn't come.

John believed that Lynne would 'come to her senses' sooner or later and they'd only got to wait. Maisie managed to have a few brief telephone conversations with Lynne and that was how she learned about the baby. It didn't improve relations between the two couples and Maisie felt that she had been deprived of being a grandmother. Whatever she and John thought about Jake, Dominic was their grandson and they wanted to do anything they could to help him in life. Most of all they wanted to see him.

They have applied for a contact order, and one point in their favour is that Lynne may not oppose it. Maisie's and John's chances of success are probably rather less than fifty-fifty. Their best hope is to swallow their pride and try to take Jake into their hearts.

Guardianship

This is not often applicable or useful to grandparents. Under the Children Act you can only apply to be a guardian if the child's parents are both dead, if they were married, and if not, if the responsible parent is dead. Of course, there is no need for a Court order if either of the parents had appointed you guardian in the event of their death.

Children in Care

A child is only taken into care by the local authority when something has gone disastrously wrong in the family, and the child is thought to be in danger if he or she remains there. If there are grandparents able and willing to look after the child, the Court may well conclude that it is in the child's best interest to live with them, rather than go into a home or with foster parents. The grandparents would then be given a residence order.

Pamela's daughter, Jane, married an alcoholic, a Jekyll and Hyde character. He was charming and considerate during a period of sobriety, but uncontrollably violent when he had been drinking. The granddaughter, Jessie, was disturbed by the frightening episodes of violence and made matters worse by whimpering whenever her father tried to touch her. He became increasingly angry and the day nursery staff noticed Jessie's fresh crop of bruises as well as her nervousness. Jane was afraid to cross her husband and, besides, she still loved him and kept hoping that this time he would keep his promises. The social services set off care proceedings, but in the end a residence order was granted to Pamela instead, although she was a widow on her own in a small flat.

If your grandchild is in care in a local authority home or with foster parents, and for one reason or another you cannot have him or her to live with you, you still have something of enormous value to offer. The Children Act specifically directs the authorities to do all they can to help children in care to keep in touch with their relatives, including their grandparents. The government guidance emphasizes the benefit to the child of visits if possible, however occasional, and also the value of letters, phone calls, photographs, birthday cards and presents.

As a grandmother you are special to your grandchild as no one else can be, but if you have had a long, close involvement with a child, and have acted as a grandparent, the law will recognize your importance too. This can arise if your son or daughter marries someone who already has a child whom you take to your heart although there is no tie of blood.

Any grandmother whose family is in a tangle which might involve the law would be well advised to join The Grandparents' Federation. This is a friendly, helpful organization with a wealth of information; and there is also The Family Rights Group which has a telephone help-line.

Both addresses and numbers are on p. 175

Introduction Summary

- New legal situation
- Residence orders
- Contact orders
- Effects of divorce
- Guardianship
- Children in care

Chapter 1

The News Breaks

D<small>EPENDING UPON</small> whether you are a Liz or a Val – see p. 2 (see p. 2) – this is the moment you have been longing for or dreading, or it may catch you totally by surprise. Whichever way, it is momentous news. Like marriage, this alters your status at a stroke, and there is no divorce from being a grandmother. It's for life.

If it is your daughter who is the mother-to-be, she will probably tell you herself. If it is your daughter-in-law, your son may break the news. It is vital to check with him if his wife – or girlfriend – knows that he is telling you and whether you are meant to know. You'll be flooded with a muddle of emotions, including some anxiety about the practical aspects. What will be expected of you? But for the moment, all that matters is your response. If you've any worries or reservations, keep them well out of sight.

For the mother, this is something magical, marvellous and a little frightening. Already she feels protective towards her baby. She will take the smallest indication of lukewarmness as a sign of hostility towards the precious innocent. So: you must be wonderstruck, congratulatory, happy and optimistic. This is no time for casting doubts, criticizing or asking searching questions. Act as though this were the best news in the world, even if:

- your daughter-in-law has a good job and her salary is essential to the couple's standard of living
- the father has been made redundant or is still a student
- their accommodation – bedsit with shower – is miserably inadequate
- your son's career will be ruined by this thoughtless girl's

11

landing him with the responsibility and expense of a child, at this stage
- your daughter's career will be ruined by this selfish man's thoughtlessness in wanting a family now

These are all commonplace situations which you have to take on board. None of them is a disaster, and there will be plenty of time later for plans and adjustments. These, of course, are the couple's affair, but you may be drawn in and consulted. Wait and see.

SPECIAL CIRCUMSTANCES

Sometimes there are more serious problems – like Emil, the son-in-law who didn't want to be a parent, and Sammie, a problem teenager. Here are their stories:

Emil, Daphne's boyfriend, was French. They had been living together on and off for two years, so it was no flash in the pan affair. Daphne was thirty-two. Emil was the same age, but did not have a biological clock. He was appalled by the spectre of compulsory domesticity replacing their carefree, pleasure-filled life. He was convinced that, for their future happiness, Daphne should have a termination. He would take her on a holiday in La Napoule to get over it.

Daphne had not forgotten the Pill on purpose, though Dr Freud might have blamed her unconscious, but now that she knew she was pregnant she wanted the baby. Emil's views didn't budge and finally he issued an ultimatum: if Daphne went ahead and had the baby, it was all over between them. Daphne's mother was faced with the question: 'What shall I do, Mum?' She had never much liked Emil, but there was no doubt that he made Daphne happy and the couple shared an interesting and exciting life.

One thing was certain: whatever Daphne said, her mother must not do any of the deciding. All she could do – and this was extremely valuable – was to encourage Daphne to talk about her feelings and to assure her of support, whichever course she chose. In the end Daphne decided to keep the baby, hoping that Emil would come round. He hasn't.

Laura's stepdaughter, Sammie, had been through a long, difficult patch. She was smoking cigarettes at twelve, cannabis at fourteen, drinking alcohol at fifteen and then into raves and at least one experiment with Ecstasy at sixteen. Over the last two years, thankfully, she seemed to have settled down. It was an unexpected jolt when Sammie broke it: a very much unplanned one-night indiscretion and the boy didn't have a condom. Sammie thought it would be OK, just once.

Laura felt her anger rising: this was past the limit. Then she looked at the girl's pale face, and remembered herself aged eighteen being scared in a similar situation. She was able to bite back the criticism and was surprised to hear herself sounding understanding and supportive. She offered to soften Sammie's father Ed's attitude before Sammie spoke to him. It is often better for family harmony in these circumstances for the wife to help the girl's father to adjust to the situation ahead of any father/daughter confrontation.

In this case, it all worked for the best. What had been a spiky relationship between Sammie and Laura ever since her marriage to Ed began to melt into feminine fellow-feeling. Laura found herself looking forward to experiencing with her (step) grandchild much of what she had missed by having no children of her own.

PREGNANCY UNDER WAY

In general this is a happy period, with the prospect of a new family member bringing fresh hope and interest, but like everything to do with being a grandmother, you have to tread carefully. If the mother-to-be is experiencing the wretched waves of nausea that can plague the first three months, your sympathy, as another woman, is like balm. A ready supply of plain biscuits, and your reassurance that this is a temporary phase only, will be appreciated. Nevertheless, however well-meaning you may be, beware of these traps:

- pointing out to the parents-in-waiting that it may harm their baby if they smoke and drink: they know

- asking about early nights, a sensible diet and vitamins: this will be seen as fussing
- hi-jacking the fun by buying or knitting baby gear, following your own ideas. Take the mother with you on any shopping trip so that she can choose what she needs. With knitting, don't even begin until you have had clearance re colour, style and yarn
- giving any indication of what you hope for, of course regarding sex, but also such remarks as these: 'I hope he'll turn out clever like his father,' or '. . . inherits Susie's looks.'

WHAT ABOUT YOU?

While you may bend over backwards to do and say the right thing for the other people, as a grandmother-to-be your feelings need consideration, too. You are entering a new, unknown phase of your life. You may welcome it whole-heartedly and a little sentimentally. Even so, little anxieties creep in. Your friends who are already grandparents are good company in this situation.

More likely you are bewildered, uncertain how you will fit into a granny role. You may feel much too young, at heart as well as chronologically. These days being old starts at around eighty-five. Grandfathers-to-be can find it unpalatable to be so labelled. If your partner is one such, he needs reassurance that he is young, attractive and as sexy as ever. My father was fifty-one when I first knew I was expecting. He had just embarked on his third marriage, to a woman not much older than me. There was no way he could bear the appellation 'Grandad': it would be a hideous insult. He had always preferred me to call him by his first name; clearly my child must be taught to do the same.

If you are a working woman or otherwise busy, you may be afraid that either you'll be seen as a bad grandmother or else you'll be worn to irritability by trying to put double the activity into your twenty-four hours – with baby-minding and the like. Gradually, a workable plan will evolve, but meanwhile give yourself – and your partner or a friend – a few adult treats plus a new outfit to celebrate a new role.

DOUBTS AND DISABILITIES

Are you up to the job physically? We are not all the young, thrusting executive type with energy for forty-eight hours packed into every twenty-four. Suppose, for instance, you have arthritis – it caught me absolutely by surprise – or some other problem that restricts your mobility? It is a positive advantage with the small-sizers: your speed suits their short legs. Any difficulty or disability you may have can make a child of any age feel important. How splendid to be needed to pick something up for Gran, because she can't bend down, or to fetch her something from upstairs. An older grandchild may even go to the library or to a shop, with money, for you. They will like feeling 'big'.

Teenagers, especially, appreciate a static grandmother: one who is always available to sit and talk, rather than dashing off to work or a committee meeting, or just 'too busy' to listen with love and care. The art of being a grandparent is not competing with the parents, but adding something special that only a more senior generation can provide.

SNEAK PREVIEW: WHAT IT FEELS LIKE TO BE A GRANDMOTHER

The Agony and the Ecstasy is the evocative title of a book about grandparents (and religion). Certainly your emotions get caught up in your grandchild's welfare. The joy can be intense when your grandchild wins a race or does well in GCSEs. Your anxiety when the little one is ill or unhappy is also acute, but because you've lived through ups and downs and disasters – and come through – your perspective is more practical than panicky.

The Generation Link is the name of a project set up by Lambeth Council in inner London for surrogate grannying as a part of child welfare. In fact, they are making use of the natural trust and understanding between a child and someone of grandparent age. The generation gap which enables our own children to express their separate individuality and ultimately live apart from us parents does not apply with grandchildren. Instead, there is a mutual respect.

Lois had always been a difficult child, partly because of her asthma. At that time there weren't the drugs available to control it, which meant that she was often ill. Even more often, it seemed to her, her mother prevented her from doing something enjoyable in case it brought on an attack. Lois was resentful and rebellious as she grew up, complaining that her mother 'didn't understand'. She was a bright girl and qualified as an engineer, a job she loved. She married a colleague and when, two years later, Toby was born she determined to be a perfect modern mother as well as a career woman. Working part-time seemed an ideal arrangement.

All went well for the first two-and-a-half years. Lois's mother, Margaret, was allowed to admire her grandson, but her advice was definitely not required. Then Toby's tantrums started. He would hold his breath until he went blue, wriggle away and run off in the street, or scream and throw himself on the ground in the supermarket – if he didn't get the chocolate bar he wanted, and sometimes even if he did. None of the au pairs would stay, nor the more expensive mother's helps. Lois tried reason, smacking, threats, taking his toys away or giving him new ones. Nothing worked.

Oddly enough, Toby didn't often have an outburst on the few occasions that Lois trusted him to his Nan. He would snuggle onto her knee and together they would point out the people and animals in his book, or he would walk along holding her hand while they talked, stopping whenever there was something interesting to see. It might take half an hour to go round the big pond or down the High Street. Partly it was the pace and the absence of any tension or urgency that calmed him down, but most of all it was that the small boy and his grandmother were in tune with each other, naturally.

Margaret had never managed to achieve this harmony with her daughter. When Lois was a child their relationship had been shot through with worry on the one side and defiance on the other. With Toby, Margaret didn't have the anxious need to take control she'd had with Lois. After all, Lois had grown out of her asthma in the end. It is much easier to enjoy the

*relationship with a grandchild if you don't take over the
mother's role. Margaret didn't.*

Your stake in the future is suddenly much broader and more
interesting when you become a grandmother. There is a whole
new range of subjects that are now of intense personal concern to
you, including some that were relevant when your children were
young.

- **Education** matters again. Your son or daughter and
  partner may have definite ideas, but they will be glad of
  an opportunity to talk about the subject. If you have
  views, be circumspect: advice will be interpreted as
  interference, and too much help with any fees may
  be resented.
- **The Health Service.** You are not just interested in the
  availability of hip replacements, but in the whole gamut
  of baby and school clinics, immunization, the dentist –
  and you need to be *au fait* with the infections of
  childhood that still abound.
- **Employment.** Now you have a new concern: the career
  opportunities and the state of the job market for today's
  young people.
- **Politics** may not have been of much interest, apart from
  what each party might do for pensioners. Now you must
  assess which of them is most likely to provide the mix of
  opportunity and safety-net for your children's children.
  You cannot dismiss the year 2030 as unimportant –
  every aspect of the future matters to you and yours.
- **Sex and religion** are such a minefield within families
  that you as a grandmother may find yourself the
  repository for confidences with which no one else is
  trusted. You don't have to be sitting with your knitting
  in a rocking-chair for this. Today's young grandmothers are trend-setters: wise, experienced and successful with it.

Isobel was one of the young breed of grandmothers. She worked in a small boutique and young Harry sometimes called in on his way home from school. That's how Isobel came to hear about Harry's homosexual experience and his panic in case his parents found out. Just talking and expressing his fears and feelings was a relief. It is the necessary first step towards solving any problem or at least coming to terms with it. Harry was confused by his own emotions as well as the actual events. He was only thirteen at the time, an experimenter rather than a committed gay, and the phase only lasted about nine months before he discovered girls.

Talking to Isobel helped him through a difficult time. His parents never knew: they thought he was worried about his Common Entrance exams.

In my work as a psychiatrist I have a particular interest in eating disorders, especially anorexia nervosa which affects girls of eleven upwards. In the first interview I always ask about grandmothers: they so often hold the key.

Amy was sixteen, and a worry because she weighed under six stone and was terrified of eating. Her father was the remote type of Englishman whose feelings never show, and her mother was an active do-gooder who was depressed underneath. The stress of GCSEs and A levels to come was the final trigger that pushed Amy into the starvation–exercise–homework cycle. The underlying fear which she did not understand herself was of becoming a woman, someone unhappy and unfulfilled like her mother, and with the alarming responsibilities of sexual maturing and all it entailed.

Obviously, Amy could not derive any comfort from her mother, or even confide in her. Progress with her anorexia was painfully slow: 2 lbs on then 1¾ off, in a prevailing mood of anxiety. Then her grandmother came to stay: she lived two hundred miles away. Granny Grace was now seventy-six. Arthritis had slowed down her movements, but it had also taught her patience. This is what won out with Amy. Grace did not mind how long she sat with the girl, listening when Amy felt like talking, and saying very little herself, apart from love and reassurance. It seemed so little, so gentle, yet this was the breakthrough. Once an anorexic can express her feelings in words instead of starving herself, she can begin to recover. Amy could unburden herself to Granny Grace with no fear of criticism or exhortations to 'think of her future and eat sensibly'.

- **Your money.** You may never have worried overmuch about money, so long as you had enough to live on and a little put by. Being a grandparent gives money a new importance. You may remember it being a struggle when your children were young, and perhaps having to deny them some things that you couldn't afford. It is natural to want to make it better for your grandchild and incidentally for your child and partner. Money may now mean music lessons, posh trainers, a computer – for your grandchild.

  Be careful. A spoilt child is not a happy child, but a worse danger is upstaging the parents. If you provide bigger and better, or at least, more expensive gifts than they can, the result can be resentment rather than gratitude. Your greatest value is nothing to do with money. It is generosity with your love and thoughts, and making the time you spend with your grandchild unhurried, whether it is often or occasional.

- **The fun.** Grandchildren can be maddening, demanding and exhausting but there is always the funny, touching aspect, especially when a small-sizer says in an uninhibited way what he or she thinks. My granddaughter of four has given me some delicious moments, for instance when she said that her fingers were 'sparkling': they were tingling after coming indoors on a cold day. Or when she identified a turkey as a 'chicken with a hat on its bottom'. A serious schoolboy grandson of eight had an interest in history. He asked me which side I had been on in the Wars of the Roses.

Then there is a grandchild's kindness. Robbie knows I like coffee: off his own bat he brought me a few grains of instant in lukewarm water, slopping around in the best china cup and saucer. Little Corrie was kind, kissing a worm she found in the garden because 'he was so cold and had nothing on'.

Note for Great-grandmothers

Great-grandmother: it sounds a venerable title, like a rare antique, but of course, in these days of longer life, especially for women, it is no longer a rarity. You can be a granny before you are forty if you and your son or daughter were into teenage love. At that rate, you might find yourself a great-gran by the time you get your bus pass. It is more likely that you will be nudging eighty when you have your first great-grandchild. That gives you an expectation of fifteen years as a great-grandmother.

You might think that now you are not so active physically, you are not particularly useful to the younger ones in the family. Nonsense: think of the Queen Mother, an inspiring example of a well-loved great-grandmother in her nineties. She is obviously in tune with the youngest generation, and holds a difficult family together by her warmth and serenity. Perhaps, as a caring gardener, she sees her children, grandchildren and great-grand-children like plants, which grow and develop and blossom.

Certainly you acquire a more tranquil perspective on the turbulent years of childhood when you have seen them over and over. This tranquillity and your accumulated wisdom make you a precious asset to the family. As an adviser and peace-maker you can do more of real value to those you love than all the practical, nappy-changing help in the world.

The News Breaks Summary

- Pros and cons
- Your children's partners
- During the pregnancy
- Doubts and disabilities
- Health, education and employment
- The fun bit
- Great-grandmothers

Chapter 2
Baby Days

YOU WILL NEVER be more completely a grandmother than in the weeks immediately following your grandchild's birth. You may even have been the one to take your daughter, or less likely, your daughter-in-law, to the hospital. Labour can start any time and catch you out.

Nowadays it is the father whom a mother most wants to hold her hand and share the birth with her, but sometimes he is not available – for a variety of reasons. The saddest one is that he is ducking out of all responsibility. In this situation, although a friend may be chosen, it is often her own mother that the mother-to-be wants near her. This is a time when mother and daughter experience an intense closeness, a primitive sharing of what it means to be a woman. A young mother, giving birth, often calls out for her mother, whoever else is present. This happens even when, in normal circumstances, the girl is independently minded and inclined to be disparaging about the older generation.

Remember that this new mother was your helpless baby once, and now she is frightened and needs you, although she may adopt an air of sang-froid. What you must not do, while being available as needed, is to get in the way of the baby's father around the time of the actual birth. If he is on the scene leave the stage to him, not forgetting to praise him for his part in the miracle. He will be in a state of high tension too. Men need help to feel important at this crucial time when women are so clearly the top sex.

Of course you must be in the forefront of the baby-worshippers. Absolutely everything you say must be admiring and reassuring, and reflect the pride and wonder the parents feel at having created this new human being. Don't be moved to say, however tenderly: 'Poor little scrap,' when you see the tiny, helpless creature. If the red marks of the birth journey still show on his face, ignore them. This baby is beautiful, no matter what other adjectives come to mind, and, as far as you are concerned, perfect.

AFTER-BABY BLUES
This is the common reaction of weepiness when a mother has safely come through all the effort and anxiety, and the strangeness of having a baby. Be comforting and hug the sufferer, but don't apply reason. She knows she 'ought' to feel happy, but her wave of sadness is emotional, natural and very temporary.

THE FIRST FORTNIGHT
If it is your daughter who is the mother, you may find yourself embroiled in a full-time job as baby nurse, home help and diplomat. Unless you intend to opt out and have explained this in advance, you will need to clear your diary of work or other commitments for the period. You are likely to be press-ganged into major responsibility, coupled with the lowliest menial tasks. Your daughter will expect you to be *au fait* with 1990s baby care, including any quirky ideas she has, and she will be watching you with hypercritical eyes. Your son-in-law will take you for granted – not deliberately but because he has so much that is new to think about.

The baby will snooze fitfully, cry and need changing in a non-stop, endless rhythm, but at least the modern equipment cuts down on washing. Among it all, you will experience moments of intense pleasure, but at best it is extremely exhausting; even when everything is straightforward.

Esther, at fifty-five, was not a maternal type. Harriet had been her only child and she loved her dearly, and of course she wanted the best for little Joseph. She offered to help and might have managed to get through the crucial fortnight with no more damage than one ruined suit. But there was a complication, in fact two. Her son-in-law had been a widower when he married

23

Harriet, and there were the twins to look after. They were six years old, a boy and a girl.

Esther had never got to know the twins well: she had not felt they were her concern. They were already vulnerable because of the loss of their mother, then their father's remarriage. Now the new baby rocked their world. They alternated between over-excitement and sulky withdrawal. It was clear that they were put out by the fuss over Baby Joe. Michael suggested that Joe should be 'sent back' as they didn't need him. Mandy, his sister, was cautiously interested.

Esther realized that it was the twins, not the baby, who most desperately needed lashings of love and interest in their doings – and quality time with their father. Esther struggled to change her instinctively stand-off attitude towards the pair, and tried to bring them into everything she did. She reminded Harriet to spare some of her overflowing warmth towards children for these two, although their behaviour was particularly tiresome when the baby was demanding, too. Esther thought it would be more tactful if it was Harriet, not his mother-in-law, who suggested that big Joe should reserve a special time for his older children.

Esther came through these vital, early weeks frazzled but satisfied that she had done all she could to start Harriet and her family off on the right road. It was like Heaven for Esther to slip back into her normal, busy, well-ordered routine – and a husband who had only just survived. They had never appreciated anything so much as that first peaceful weekend together.

Sometimes the situation can be the opposite of Esther's. If your son is the father, you may have a step-grandchild belonging to his wife from a previous marriage – or partnership. You may not have seen yourself as a grandmother until your son's baby came along, and had tolerated the older child kindly enough, but without warmth. In that case you have a double task: the easy part of giving your love and attention to your baby grandchild, and the difficult part of being even-handed with your show of interest – and even-hearted. Children of all ages are acutely sensitive to the emotional temperature: babies and 'big' children need to feel the warmth. For the baby's sake, apart from the humane considerations, it is happier and safer if there is no jealousy in the family.

Susan was a new grandmother with a difficult set of circumstances. She was a divorcee because of her ex-husband's wandering tendencies. She had brought Linda and Tom up on her own since they were seven and five respectively. That was ten years before. Their father had lost interest in them after the first couple of years and had virtually vanished from the scene.

Susan was a nurse and by doing extra stints of agency work had just managed to keep their finances afloat. Now she had a regular NHS job in the Outpatient Clinic and the children were both at the big comprehensive half a mile away. Linda planned to do a secretarial course after her GCSEs, and Susan felt that life was becoming easier. It didn't work out. Linda had become pregnant at sixteen and, like many other child-mothers, of course she wanted to keep the baby. Susan could sympathize: besides, it was her own flesh-and-blood, her own grandchild, in question. The father was the school caretaker, a man in his thirties with a wife and two kids already. There was no mileage there.

Linda waltzed through the pregnancy, truth to tell, rather pleased with herself. Susan took annual leave to look after Linda and the baby in the first few weeks. That part went well, but Susan was in a fair way to becoming permanently trapped. She had managed to get a night nursing post, so that she could look after the baby while Linda was at school. Of course she wanted Linda to get her GCSEs before she left school. This would be a matter of only a few months, but Susan could see herself left to bring up her granddaughter: a re-run of the wearying battle to cope when Linda and Tom were young. And the baby would lose out, without a proper relationship with her one parent.

Susan is encouraging Linda to join the local Gingerbread group: the outfit for single parents. With support from her own generation, she may be able to move out in due course. She is nearly eighteen now, and is eligible for help from the authorities. Susan loves her grandchild and does not want to come to resent her. It might have been different if Linda's father had been there, sharing the family problems.

Peta's son, James, had married Tess when he was in his final year at university. Peta was sure that it was because of the pregnancy, although James swore otherwise. Tess was a pretty, pert little thing who worked as a waitress at a local restaurant. Peta was convinced that she had deliberately ensnared her son and stolen him from the family – with no thought for his career.

The child, when it arrived, was a boy, touchingly like James when he was a baby. He captured Peta's heart, and all her pent-up emotions were focused on him, almost ignoring his young mother. Peta was generosity itself – to the baby. She poured scorn on the idea of calling him Jason: it had got to be James, like his father. He would, of course, be put down for James's old school and the prep school before that . . . Tess and James proved unexpectedly awkward.

Instead of welcoming grandparental help and showing some gratitude, they seemed to prefer to do everything themselves. They didn't even want advice about the boy's future: they had their own weird ideas. Peta felt shut out – from her own grandson – she learned the hard way that the only route to a happy relationship with him was through a happy relationship with both his parents.

BABY WORRIES

Newly-fledged parents are given to panic: if their baby breathes too noisily or too quietly, sneezes, hiccups, or regurgitates some milk. They interpret one loose motion as gastroenteritis. They need your confident reassurance that these things are normal, and that you know from experience. But beware. During the first eighteen months there will be a range of situations in which you are sure that you know best. They include:

Danger Points
Breast versus bottle
Feeding schedules: demand or by the clock
Dummies
Toilet-training: when to start
Rooming in or separately
Safety precautions: cat nets etc
Freedom or discipline
Baby talk
Parents smoking
Immunization

Unless your opinion is specifically requested, keep your views to yourself. The most that you can do is praise the young couple's wisdom if they chance to do it your way.

Glenda, as an ex-smoker, had strong convictions about the habit. She had read the newspaper reports about the dangers of passive smoking to young children. Both her son-in-law, Giles, and her daughter Fiona were smokers. Fiona had given up during her pregnancy, but now the stress of looking after this strange, precious little human being, added to the ordinary chores, had started her off again. She avoided smoking when she was feeding or changing the baby, but lit up thankfully with a coffee afterwards.

Glenda was indignant on behalf of Baby Norma. Naturally enough she blamed her son-in-law primarily. He had continued smoking moderately throughout. Criticism of Giles provoked a fierce reaction from Fiona, who pointed out that Glenda had always had a cigarette in her mouth when she was a child – was Glenda suggesting that Fiona was intellectually stunted and a physical wreck? Glenda argued feebly that in those days people didn't realize . . .

New parents are notoriously prickly over their actions and responsibilities. This is the other side of their own insecurity. Glenda abandoned her one-woman anti-smoking campaign when she found that it was wrecking the relationship with her daughter. Being right doesn't count when you are a grandparent.

NAMING THE NEW BABY

Choosing the baby's name and the ceremony that accompanies it can be a minefield of family prejudice and misunderstanding. The advent of a new baby is unlike any other human experience: a wonder and a renewal of hope for the future. Whether the family has a strong religious faith or almost none, there is a feeling of thankfulness for the infant's safe delivery and a desire that he or she should be blessed.

The majority of people in Britain are lukewarm Christians, who remember their church only for marriages, funerals — and christenings. There are no rules for ordinary C of E parents to observe in choosing their child's name, so long as it is not so outrageous that the vicar will not accept it.

Everyone in the Parker family — both sets of grandparents, two aunts and an uncle — had definite but different ideas on what Douglas and Janet's baby should be called. On Douglas's side there was a family tradition of calling the eldest child Denzil if he was a boy, Sonia for a girl. One of the spinster aunts, who was to be a godmother, put forward a passionate plea that the little girl should be called Coralie, after her. It was a charming name. Janet's mother, on the other hand, believed that a simple name, which couldn't be messed about, was the best, for instance Janet, or even Jane. Janet said that she hated her old-fashioned name and wanted Kylie, while her husband leaned towards Amy, his mother's name. The uncle suggested Danielle, because of the family's French connections.

The final choice was Kylie Danielle. All four grandparents and both aunts were disgruntled, but as Janet said, the grandparents had their turn at choosing babies' names about twenty-seven years ago.

Conscientious, practising Roman Catholics often choose saints' names for their children. This provides an ongoing benefit, as one little girl explained to me: two birthdays, one for herself and one for her saint's day, in her case, Hilary. The essential part of a christening, a Christian naming ceremony, is a symbolic cleansing with water and the introduction of the child into the community of the Church under God's protection.

Christenings and other naming ceremonies are the happiest of family occasions, and an opportunity for the grandparents from both sides to get to know each other. A warm, co-operative relationship with the other grandmother is something worth working for. Too often there is a jealous rivalry, each wanting to prove that she is the better and more popular one. What your grandchild will call you depends on your choice and what he or she finally pronounces. Granny and Nan are the commonest, but you may not feel happy with either, especially if you are too young to fit the stereotype.

If you are a Muslim, or your child has married a Muslim and adopted that faith, you may find that traditional naming customs come into play. Indeed, the moment a Muslim baby is born the first words he should hear are those of the Shahadah, the words of faith. Sometimes the Imam chooses the baby's name, if the family is strict, and such names have a religious meaning. Abdullah means 'servant of Allah' and Fardose means 'thank heaven'. For the name-giving ceremony, Aqiqar, the baby's head is shaved. A touch of honey or sugar is put on the baby's tongue, and the meat of the celebratory meal is also sweetened. Gifts are made to charity to thank Allah for the baby, and the parents have a special duty to ensure that he or she is instructed in the religion. Muslim baby boys are usually circumcised at an early age, but this is not compulsory.

Hindu babies are told the words of faith, the Mool Mantra, as soon as possible. There is a naming ceremony when he or she is ten days old, at which the letters OM or AUM are traced on the infant's tongue with honey. At one year the baby's head is shaved to get rid of the sins of past lives.

Sikhs celebrate the birth of a new baby by decorating their house. The naming takes place when the child first goes to the gurdwara. He or she is given a little sugar water, amrit, and introduced to Nam – God. The adults share a sweet pudding, kara parshad. Sugar symbolizes sweetness and purity. An indication of the best name to select comes from the granth or holy book.

Jewish baby boys are circumcised at eight days old at a ceremony called Brit Milah from which grandmothers and all women are excluded. A prayer of blessing, the kiddush, is said and those present drink some wine. The baby also has a sip of wine and he is then named. The baby, men and boys then rejoin the rest of the family. It is less complicated for baby girls, and nowadays most young Jewish couples prefer the simpler services of the reformed church to strict orthodox practices.

All these naming ceremonies help to bind the wider family across generations. Particularly if you are of a different faith from Christianity, as a grandparent you are likely to know the rules and traditions better than the younger generation. You may have to show them the way. With a multicultural society, some of us will find that our child may marry someone with a different religion from our own. It is as well to know what the form is for naming, and to remember that this is for the baby and the parents. Grandmothers are members of the supporting cast.

The Other Grandparents

When your child got married you probably met the other parents for the first time. Everyone was dressed up to the nines, which is often the opposite of comfortable and relaxed. Your opposite number's fixed smile may have had something to do with a pinching shoe, and you may have been wishing you had your thermals on underneath the smart gear. Nevertheless, you all got through the day and the young couple set off, leaving everyone exhausted.

You may not have seen anything of the other family after that, although there could be a little rivalry over Christmas. It is when a grandchild appears on the scene that the real interaction begins. This is even more the case when the 'children' have dispensed with ceremony and just moved in together. Methods of child care and choosing a name are among the early hurdles: but it is the parents who have the final say. Your son or daughter chose his or her partner. No way is it a love match between you and that other lot of grandparents.

We all think that we are ordinary, and everyone else a little out-of-line. Every family is special, with special values, special ways of doing things. Since your grandchild is someone else's grandchild too, it is important that these natural differences don't lead to an 'atmosphere' – or worse. The two sets of grandparents don't have to be in each other's pockets, but you do need to try and see the situation from the other side's viewpoint.

One cast-iron rule is that, whatever you think, you never say anything derogatory about the other family: they are now your child's – and your grandchild's – family as well. There may be divergences of outlook depending on whether you come from a city or a country background, the sturdy North or the romantic West Country. Politics can divide people in the same nuclear family, and even more when two families are brought together by their children.

> *The Taylors were quite happy when their son fell in love with Shanti. It was when the baby was born and Shanti's parents Raju and Shireen came over from Bombay to see him that the gulf between them and the Taylors seemed so huge. All four grandparents were sensible and adult: they knew that one of the best ways of discussing difficult matters is over a shared meal.*
>
> *The Taylors and the Lams enjoyed a multicultural meal, each appreciating the other's dishes and learning more about their different beliefs and lifestyles. And the successful blend of cultures was confirmed by the baby's name: Alan Ram Taylor.*

THE MOST WONDERFUL SHOW IN THE WORLD

Whether you are popping in and out every day or can only visit your grandchild from time to time, as a grandmother you have a grandstand view of the miraculous changes and delicious, absurd moments of your grandchild's babyhood. As a mother, you were probably too caught up with the day-to-day practicalities to enjoy it to the full.

Thelma lives a hundred miles from her son and his wife. When Baby Emma was born, Thelma promised herself not to miss out. It was difficult to get away from her demanding job, helping her husband, Brian, run his small building firm. She could only envisage making the trip about once every month or six weeks. She decided to make a record of each visit, so that she could enjoy them over again. These are Thelma's notes for the first year and a half.

First sight: Jilly looked a little wan, but so proud when she introduced me to my granddaughter, one day old. They planned to call her Emma. She was 19 inches long and weighed 6 lbs 12 oz (just over 3 kg if you are into metric) when she was born. She looked too heart-breakingly fragile to be out in this big, bright, noisy world, having to do her own breathing and work for the nourishment which had been supplied automatically in the womb.

Her tiny fists were closed, thumbs inside, and her eyes, when she opened them, were that deep, dark blue that only babies have. I know she could not yet make much sense of what she saw, but her straight gaze made me feel that she could see right through to my soul, since she had so recently come from Heaven. Of course she has everything to learn. A door banged along the corridor and Emma jumped – not just her shoulders, like us, but all over, including her arms and legs. Then she cried and Jilly let me hold her, snugly wrapped in a shawl, and I tried to make my arms convey how precious she is. She sighed and stopped crying. I felt as though I had been given a hundred pounds.

One month: this weekend I saw Emma. She was awake, lying on her back with one arm outstretched and her head turned to that side: this is her favourite position, Jilly told me. I wonder if it means that she's right-handed? When I came into her line of vision she gave me an intent look and her eyes followed me briefly when I moved. So – she has already learned to use the twelve minute muscles that control each eye. She has also learned to swallow efficiently in rhythm with her feeding: newborn babies already have the knack of sucking (they practise before they are born), but need to fine-tune their swallowing technique now they have to cope with real milk. Before now, almost as much would run out of Emma's mouth, at times, as she kept in.

I know she likes me talking to her, because if she's grumbling to herself, the sound of my voice makes her stop. She can't talk back to me but she can make comfortable little throaty noises as well as the alarm call of crying. She can sneeze and blink and cough, but what I especially liked was to see her yawn – just like an adult. Another clever trick Emma is mastering is how to use her face muscles to make a smile, although she can't do it at any particularly appropriate time yet.

While last month I felt that Emma was hardly mature enough to be born (she came within two days of the expected date), now I feel she is ready to live in our world. I'm grateful she's here.

Two months: I wasn't able to get down to London this month, but Jilly tells me that I would be amazed at how much Emma has grown. Apparently she is more than 2 lbs (1 kg) heavier than when she was born, and nearly 2 inches (5 cm) longer. That must have been difficult to measure! The nicest bit is that now, instead of gazing through Jilly, she definitely meets her eye and smiles as though she means it. She also looks as though she wants to reach out for her rattle and makes a kind of struggle, but her arms won't co-operate yet.

Three-and-a-half months: Emma can laugh, and I am enchanted by her wide, gummy smile. I am sure she can recognize me, and we can both enjoy our conversations. I tell her anything that comes to mind about what I am doing, while she has a repertoire of squeals and cooing and gurgles and chuckles, as well as blowing bubbles through her lips. Sometimes she 'talks' to herself and seems so interested in the process that she hardly notices anyone else. I brought my camera this time, and have taken a good shot of her lying on her tummy and holding her head up. She can manage this for all of ten seconds.

Jilly says that from her point of view the most important advance Emma has made is in sleeping through the night, more often than not now. Sizewise she has not quite reached double her birthweight, as the books lead you to expect. So long as she is feeding and sleeping OK, and seems happy and lively, I am sure it doesn't matter. Babies are like flower buds opening and developing at their own individual pace.

(*Author's note: My two eldest grandchildren were standard size babies, but after that they were noticeably smaller than other people's children of the same age. The paediatrician told my daughter and son-in-law not to worry. Now Harry, at thirteen, is taller than either of his parents, and Chloë looks about average among the other new students. Except that I think she is prettier and cleverer.*)

Four-and-a-half months: last time I saw Emma she could only hold her rattle if I put it in her hand. She used to make a wobbly swipe at it but couldn't get it in her grasp. Now she uses a determined, two-handed approach – and can take it straight to her mouth. She puts everything to the test in this fashion, and often sucks her knuckle for pleasure.

She has found her toes are interesting to see and play with, but she is even more fascinated by her hands. She looks at them and touches one with the other. She is curious about everything round her. Emma's head is not nearly as wobbly and she can half sit up with help. She loves to be propped up enough to get a good view of what's going on. She likes playing Peep-Bo with me and laughs aloud with the fun of it.

I hated having to leave.

Six months: Emma's half birthday. She's got a new outfit, since she had grown out of all her baby clothes. She can sit up with only a little support, although she slides down, tired, after a short time. She isn't exactly saying Mama and Dada yet, but she's on the way. She goes 'mumumum . . .' and 'bababa . . .' but can't do 'dadada'. I think 'gagaga' as practice for Granny involves an even more difficult consonant, so I shall have to be patient.

Emma certainly knows Jilly and John (her father) and me, but she is most delighted when she catches sight of Bonnington, the family cat. You can tell by her expression that Emma understands 'No' and 'naughty' and 'good girl'. She has been dribbling a lot lately and biting her toys, so I guess she has some teeth on the way. The two middle ones at the bottom usually come through somewhere between the fifth and seventh months, so I expect this is the last time she will smile at me with her gums. I am so glad it is summer, as she is less likely to get the miserable cough and snuffle that sometimes accompanies teething.

Emma's favourite toy at the moment is a string of big, bright, wooden beads. She also made a grab at my necklet of shiny pretend pearls. Her second favourite is a little pink woolly rabbit with a tinkling bell inside.

Nine months: Emma has six teeth now: four at the bottom and two at the top. It means that she can bite a chocolate finger and you have to be careful that she doesn't choke with the crumbs. Of course she can sit up by herself, but what is much more exciting – she can crawl. Up till now she made a great effort with her arms and legs when she was on her tummy, but did not actually travel an inch. Now she has invented a half sitting, half crawling manoeuvre, which means you have to watch her all the time. She can reach everything, everywhere at ground level.

Her best toys are rollers and balls of all colours and sizes to roll across the floor and follow. Jilly's pots and pans come second. Emma enjoys taking the lids off and banging them down. She often tries to pull herself up to standing, but falls down partway: this is a joke. Another joke was getting hold of my specs. She is interested in faces, and sometimes pats both my cheeks, softly and lovingly, but she may suddenly decided to investigate my eye.

For the first time, Emma showed signs of shyness. This was not with me, thank goodness, but when one of Jilly's friends came in for coffee and innocently went across to say 'Hello', Emma's face crumpled. The visitor was wearing a smart black suit, the colour that babies like least. Pink is their first choice.

One year: this was one party I wouldn't have missed for a thousand pounds. Emma was as proud as Punch, sitting at the table in her clip-on chair. It is so much safer than the high chairs my little ones used. She looked like a princess with a ribbon tying a tuft of her scanty, shiny gold hair and a proper little girl's dress, instead of the pint-sized dungarees she usually wears. Apart from the adults, Emma had a friend to share her birthday tea – a little boy of eighteen months, who can walk and sit on a grown-up chair. Emma was obviously interested. She herself has a new way of getting around: on her hands and feet. It is very fast, but she is wanting to stand up and walk. She can do it holding my hand, with a wide drunken gait.

Now she can throw a ball, or a brick or a spoon, and leave go when she wants to. A favourite game is picking up toys or anything else to hand and dropping them onto the floor. She likes to see where they finish up. I have found that it is a mistake to laugh or she will do it all the more, for instance with the shopping. They say that when a baby can leave go with her hand when she wants, she is ready for serious potty training. I leave all that to Jilly to decide, unless she asks. You have to be super-tactful as a mother-in-law.

Emma was intrigued by her cake and the one flickering candle, but she could not understand about blowing it out. She cried when a helpful adult succeeded in extinguishing it, so it had to be lit again. She could easily, if messily, manage a piece of cake and a biscuit by herself. She could hold a spoon and bang it into the dish of jammy rice pudding which she likes, but it was too complicated to scoop up a spoonful and get the whole thing in her mouth right way up.

Emma has almost mastered drinking from a mug, and can manage the last bit by herself. She usually puts the mug upside down then. She likes to rattle a spoon in an empty mug. Bibs don't really work, so there is lots more for the washing machine these days.

Emma knows her name and looks round when she hears it. She talks a lot to herself, these days, while she is playing. It sounds like a conversation, but there are a lot of made-up words strung together. She says 'Emmie' probably because we do. She can also say 'Bye-bye' and wave when Jilly asks her to. When she was safely ensconced on Jilly's knee she said 'Bye-bye' loudly and clearly to the lady in black who had come to visit again, and was showing no signs of leaving. Emma still prefers her mother to be at hand when there are strangers around.

Another new skill Emma has learned is the use of her first finger. She explores all holes and crannies with it, picks up tiny things, such as crumbs, in conjunction with her thumb – and she uses it to point imperiously at what she wants.

Fifteen months: Emma can build a house: that is, balancing one coloured brick on top of another. She tried three but that went wrong. She can walk by herself now and especially likes to push a little cart with a handle, with all her toys piled up in it. She reminds me of those old ladies who use their shopping trolleys to steady themselves.

Linked with walking, I think, is an awareness of when she is wet. She points and says something that sounds like 'Oh dear' when she has made a puddle, but it is always too late. Her favourite toys are quite sophisticated: all the push and pull types, a doll with cot and pram, and cardboard or plastic-covered books. She is delighted with games and phrases like 'Eeny meeny miney mo' and 'Fee fie fo fum' and she has some of her own, such as 'Foggie oggie goggie'. She likes to look at other children, but there isn't any co-operative play yet.

Eighteen months: this seems to be a language stage. Emma knows lots of words. She can point to her eyes or her nose, if you ask, and knows dog, cat, car and ball, among other pictures in her books. She likes to do a round-and-round scribble as a picture, on any available surface. Although she understands much more than she can say, she has acquired some useful expressions. She frequently says 'No' and 'mine', and now she often says 'Oh dear' before she is wet, so that she is dry for long periods.

She is able to manage her first sentences: 'Gimme ball,' 'What's dat?' and 'I good girl.' Emma is not a baby any more. She is a toddler.

Baby Days Summary

- Crunch point
- After-baby blues
- First fortnight
- When not to know best
- Names and naming ceremonies
- The other grandparents
- First birthday

Chapter 3
Terrible Toddlers

THIS IS WHEN being a grandmother really has a punch. Your grandchild, the helpless little bundle that was, is now firmly on his feet, fully mobile and full of ideas. If you are entrusted with keeping an eye on the toddler, even for half-an-hour, beware. You cannot relax for a second. Only last weekend, while my daughter slipped out of the room to make us some tea, I was left with my dear little grandson of nineteen months. In a flash, with a merry smile, he had posted a biscuit into the video recorder. My son-in-law spent the rest of the weekend taking the recorder apart and then reassembling it, minus biscuit.

It is during this delightful, cute, infuriating stage from eighteen months to school that you are most likely to be asked to look after your grandchild. The parents, by this time, are desperate for a break. They've been on duty twenty-four hours a day all these months. You may have done some baby-sitting in the early stages, but this is something else.

You are dealing with an adolescent: not the painful, confusing transition from child to adult, but the equally disturbing metamorphosis from baby to independent human being. The new person is an explorer, as intrepid as they come, except that every now and then she, or he, wants her mother, and to be looked after again.

NEW BABY
There may be a major complication. When the first child is two or three it is not an unusual time for a new baby to arrive. This significant family event is likely to have an impact on you as a

grandmother. Even if you are normally busy beavering away at your job, you are prone to get press-ganged, not least by your own feelings, into agreeing to look after the toddler during the crucial period when your daughter or daughter-in-law is *hors de combat.*

Your grandchild's panicky longing for her mother's undivided concern can be a problem, especially if you are a granny who only visits now and then. Your attention and generosity may cut no ice when it is someone even more familiar that he or she craves. It may not be the full drama of a new arrival: you may be kind – or foolhardy – enough to offer to have the youngster for a few nights, when the parents want at least a weekend free from childcare.

Your grandchild may know your house quite well and love visiting, but unless he or she is truly confident with you and knows your place intimately, it is safer to look after him in his own home. The familiar surroundings, not just a favourite cuddly toy, help a child to feel safe, although Mummy and Daddy aren't there. Wherever you and your grandchild may be, you need to be well versed in his precise bedtime ritual, the times and types of his meals, his bed, walk and rest times. Sometimes the toddler's mother has been having difficulties in establishing a workable routine, and she has the neat idea that you will be able to get the rebel into the swing of going to bed on the dot and eating up her healthy spinach. Or you yourself may think this is an opportunity to bring sensible order into chaos. Forget such ambitions: you will not be able to re-educate a child who already feels strange and insecure.

WHAT YOU CAN EXPECT OF A TODDLER

While his muscles are much stronger, and he enjoys every opportunity of using them, communication is unsatisfactory for both sides. Your grandchild may speak in a language that only those who live with him all the time can understand – and then not always. The frustration for a two-year-old who cannot convey his urgent needs to an adult may turn into a tantrum or refusal to eat. Speaking is so complicated. There are all those consonants which may seem like tongue-twisters, especially y, s, t, d, f, r or th. Some phrases are easy to understand: 'What dis?' or 'Who dat?', but 'Argy' doesn't make you think of 'Georgie'. Even worse are the words with no consonants, like 'o . . . ee' for doggy. But time is on your side. By the time he is three-and-a-half your grandchild may have a vocabulary of nearly a thousand words and will have mastered the trickier bits of pronunciation.

Toileting is an aspect that is likely to slip out of gear when you are temporarily in charge. Expect and prepare for any number of accidents. Don't be fazed by them. Most mothers tell everyone that their children are drier and cleaner than they really are, but anyway, in any unusual situation, this is one of the first controls to go.

A toddler is like an April day: bubbling over with sunshiny fun one moment and utterly distraught and wet at both ends the next.

GRANDFATHERS

Although in theory they are proud, and speak of the child's future, grandfathers are rarely involved until the toddler stage. Not for them the hands-on procedures of nappy-changing, or bathing a baby who is as slippery as a piece of soap and hasn't even the strength to sit up. But once the darling granddaughter or hope-for-the-future grandson is cruising around on his or her own two feet, and saying imperiously 'Mine', grandfathers are hooked.

It is not surprising, when you remember how much sport means to men. During years two and three the youngster learns to kick a ball, at first with a funny straight-legged movement, but by year three with a proper kick. This involves knee as well as hip. He or she also begins to get the hang of playing ball – throwing and the much more difficult catching. It needs to be a big, soft, bright-coloured ball to start with, to make it easier for the learner to look at the ball and check what his or her hands are doing, simultaneously.

Construction work is also a favourite with males of all ages. The senior generation becomes interested and involved when the child is old enough to handle those fiddly little Lego pieces, usually some time after the third birthday. Many little boys are especially good at this, while girls are often way ahead with words. Looking at picture books on Granpy's knee and being read to become the treasured memories of grandchildren who have grown up. Grandfathers can be very good at telling stories, different from the re-run of the old nursery tales.

Patience is an essential when you have a two- to four-year-old in tow, to cope with the endless flow of questions. The first questions are easy to answer: the what, who and where group. 'Who dat man?' 'Where Teddy?' At age three an average, healthy youngster asks around three hundred and eighty questions a day! And they get more complicated all the time, with endless hows and whys and whens: 'Why do people die?' 'Why has that lady got such a big tummy?' 'How do babies get out?' We are told that we must answer a child's questions without hesitation, simply and truthfully. Try that in the queue at the supermarket checkout . . .

We all look back on ourselves as children and on our own child's early days through the rose-tinted glass of time. This can mean that we are shocked when four-letter words fall from the lips of today's innocents. 'Oh shit, not again!' said the curly-haired cherub of four. She was playing with her baby doll, one that cries and wets itself. She spoke in just her mother's tone of voice. I expect I said damn or blast when my children were young, but of course I don't remember. It certainly isn't naughty when a little one at the stage of soaking up new vocabulary like blotting paper uses the words he or she hears.

It is a warning never to say anything in a toddler's hearing that you don't want broadcast. One occasion when everyone concerned wanted to sink through the floor was when Lucy's Spanish grandmother came over for a rare visit. 'My mummy doesn't like you,' she said and compounded it by adding: 'I don't much either.' The granny caught her breath and had the presence of mind to say 'That's all right, I like you enough for both.'

You may not agree with the practice, applied by most young parents I know, of letting even the smallest child stay up as long as he or she can keep awake – enhancing or wrecking, according to your viewpoint, the adults' evening meal and conversation. Inevitably the youngster gets tired and often peevish and needs to be put to bed, a chunk out of the middle of the evening. You can see that your grandchild is overtaxed, but whatever your opinion, keep it under wraps. You are the father-in-law of one or other parent and tact must be your middle name.

Spoiling

Ninety per cent of the time, throughout the toddling and pre-school stages, you will be enchanted by your grandchild. It is a delight to earn a smile and a hug from giving her some little toy, or making him wide-eyed with wonder by a big present at Christmas. It's a pleasure to see your grandchild wearing something that you chose and bought. Your granddaughter may look sweet in the little smocked dress you got for her – instead of the unisex dungarees her mother usually buys. And of course you intercede on the little darling's behalf when his parents are cross. He – she – is only a baby, after all, and wouldn't have known it was wrong to take the matches. Watch it!

Be careful about being helpful at meal-times, with a toddler who won't eat. You may think it's encouraging to taste a little of the lovely rice pudding and put the rest of the spoonful into young Hopeful's mouth. A hygiene-freak daughter-in-law may be out-raged. Of course she doesn't think you have AIDS – but sharing a spoon may seem too intimate, like taking the toddler into your bed. You have to be very sure what the parents, especially the mother, feel first.

As with spoiling in general, you are stealing the young mother's perks and privileges by what she sees as over-closeness. You can cause enormous unhappiness if you seem kinder, more under-standing and give better presents than the actual parents. If you are very keen that your grandchild should have, for instance, a rocking horse or a visit to Eurodisney, you should arrange it through his mother and father. The pleasure will engulf grand-child, parents and yourself, unless what you wanted was the kudos. Competing for a child's affection simply doesn't work, apart from teaching him or her to value people on the basis of material benefit.

Love is good – all are agreed – but the way that you express it can be harmful. Danger areas for loving grandparents include:

- deferring to the child's wishes all the time. In fact, having to make too many decisions can be more tiring than pleasurable
- gifts: too many take the sparkle of surprise out of all of them; too complicated leaves no room for imagination; too expensive means trouble if it is broken
- protection: 'Be careful,' 'Mind' and the like sap a little one's courage and confidence: qualities she'll need in the big, bad world outside
- threats about not loving a child if he is 'naughty' – which often means inconvenient to the adults. These devalue love itself, which cannot be switched off so easily
- treating bad behaviour as though it is funny or interesting

PERSONALITIES

Each baby has a distinct personality from the day he or she is born, but it is at the toddler stage that individuality blossoms. My friend's granddaughter will grow up to be a Lady Bountiful. She insists on giving her toys away to the other three-year-olds in the playgroup. My friend is not as appreciative as she should be of Janie's generous nature, especially when she sees her passing on the new toy she has just been given. Young Ben, on the other hand, will be the strong, silent type: he works stolidly with his construction set, his face puckered with concentration.

It's fascinating to have this preview of the sort of person your grandchild will grow up to be. It is useful, too, for judging what he or she will most enjoy. For starters, if he is an outgoing extrovert he will revel in noisy, boisterous games, but if she is a thoughtful introvert she may prefer the quiet, scientific excitement of growing mustard and cress, for a cress sandwich later.

Charles, at three, was a tense, highly-strung boy, constantly on the move, into everything and given to shrieking with excitement. He reacted with noisy crying if he was hurt, however slightly, but worst of all, he was never ready to go to bed. Even after he was put to bed he would still be awake when his parents went up at about eleven. In the morning he was jumping about on his bed or running round his room from 5 am. His meals were a nightmare, as he was always wriggling away from the table, and there was no such thing in his repertoire as playing quietly with his toys for more than a minute or two. He was an exhausting child.

'Hyperactive' – his parents said, and spoke of minimal brain damage, food additives or whatever else was the latest buzz. Oddly enough, he always seemed calmer when his Nan came. What he needed was a change in the highly charged family atmosphere. His father and mother were both quick-moving, high-achieving, dynamic types whose voices rose to shrillness during their animated discussions. When they tried to deal with Charles they added to the tension and excitement of the situation. Charles didn't need a doctor, a dietician or a neurologist: Vera, his Nan, had the key.

She was a competent woman in her fifties, with a career in ceramics, and good at sizing people up. She could see that the only way to benefit her grandson was by helping his parents to moderate their frenetic lifestyle and build more leisure slots into their schedule. Vera herself could not often take Charles off their hands, but it would be a sensible investment for them to pay a properly qualified minder to give them some times without their son, so that they could learn to relax. Charles needed occupying, but not stimulating.

Letty's temperament was a complete contrast to Charles. She was a 'good' child, quiet and thoughtful, apparently content to play by herself for hours: no bother. Her parents were comparatively mature. Janine was thirty-seven, Basil forty-four, when Letty was born. She was their first, and they had been trying to have a baby for several years. They were both devoted to Letty and very protective. Their home was equipped with gates and bars against accidents, and since they didn't want to risk their daughter catching an illness, she didn't go out if it was wet or cold, and never into crowded places. Letty did not join a playgroup for the same reason.

Letty had her toys, a generous selection, but her constant companion was Bunky, a very big dog who could talk, but only to Letty. There were no family pets because of possible allergies or germs. Bunky was an imaginary animal, not unusual among only children. But Letty's granny was worried because the little girl was so absorbed in her pretend playmate that she avoided real children and seemed nervous of them. She was due to start school in just over a year, and although she knew her letters – Janine was proud of this – she was totally unprepared for life in the classroom.

Granny knew that it was not more toys or more attention from the grown-ups that Letty needed, but some way of meeting and mixing with other pre-schoolers. Letty's mother finally agreed to the little girl accepting a gift from her granny – of dancing lessons. It was a start.

SLEEP

It is exhausting enough at the best of times, coping with a lively toddler. When a mother does not even have the respite of good nights of sleep, her nerves are apt to become ragged.

Marion's grandson, Giles, had – and was – a sleep problem. He didn't sleep and nor did anyone else in the household. It had started off with teething and continued on and off ever since. Giles was now two. It was time-consuming hard work getting him to settle to sleep, but what was worse was the night-waking. The doctor found no signs of infection in Giles' nose, throat or ear: a common cause for a child's waking several times in the night. Childish anxieties, for instance about separation if the mother is ill or returns to work for the first time after the child's birth, can lead to poor sleep. The impact of a baby brother or sister is a potent cause of disturbed nights, as well as a range of other behavioural difficulties.

None of these applied in young Giles' case, and the family was beset by fatigue and rowing. Marion wanted to help, but had no idea how. Suddenly she remembered reading some-where that 'maternal stress' was the commonest cause of a toddler's night-waking. She knew that her daughter was fretted by the hand-to-mouth shortage of money and the fact that with Colin's job as a salesman on commission they never knew how much he would earn. And the damp patch on the kitchen ceiling was getting worse. Marion couldn't alter the job market, and sympathy by itself only tends to make the recipient feel more hopeless.

Counselling, on the other hand, if it is competent, builds confidence and points the way to a constructive response to difficulties. Marion tried to put the idea into her daughter's head, as the modern approach to life – the Americans have been doing it for years. Struggling on in silence was the way of the old, square generation – Marion's. Even if the family stresses don't disappear, they may not seem so overwhelming. Many NHS GPs have counsellors among their ancillary staff.

EATING DISORDERS

Like sleeping problems, those to do with meal-times more often apply to the two and three-year-olds than children of four.

Aileen had never had a wonderful appetite, but now, at two-and-a-quarter, her favourite expression was 'Not nice'. It had reached the point where her meals seemed to occupy three-quarters of the day. She was in the dawdling stage over everything: not uncommon or abnormal, but torture to a busy mother with a hundred and one things to do. Of course, Aileen's eating problem might have reflected some deep-seated need to keep her mother or a substitute close to her, but none of the standard causes of insecurity was in evidence.

Aileen had just developed a bad habit. Being cross or over-persuasive, reward or punishment – none of these worked. Aileen's grandmother, Sybil, decided to try out her own method when she had arranged to have her little granddaughter for a weekend. The days comprised big doses of fresh air, even if it was raining, and something interesting to do after each meal. Sybil's meal plan, dredged up from the days when her own children were young, was this:

1. *A choice of two things (never more): for instance carrot or spinach, toasted or plain?*
2. *No one else in the room at meal-times except Aileen and her 'Gan'.*
3. *Little platefuls.*
4. *Two courses.*
5. *Occasionally Sybil might fill Aileen's spoon, but she never tried to spoon the food into the child's mouth.*
6. *Ten minutes maximum for each course, then the plate removed without comment, and the next activity begun.*
7. *Regular meal-times and no extras, whether or not the previous meal had been eaten.*
8. *Now and again, as a treat, Aileen could help with the cooking: the dish was bound to be delicious.*

A weekend isn't long, but the signs were hopeful enough for Sybil to hand the formula on to her daughter, gift-wrapped with tact, in case she should want to try it.

STUTTERING

Dot was worried, so were her son and daughter-in-law. Little Simon had started stuttering and at times seemed unable to get any proper sound out at all. His parents foresaw a career crippled by an inability to communicate, teasing at school and a lifetime of social embarrassment. Simon was a bright, lively lad of two-and-three-quarters, interested in everything and into everything. He had so much to say and as yet hadn't command of enough words to express it all.

This is a normal phase that affects many intelligent youngsters at this age. The stuttering sometimes lasts only a few weeks, but more often two or three months. It is only likely to persist if an atmosphere of anxiety builds up whenever the child speaks. Nagging, encouraging, finishing his sentences, showing concern and discussing the problem in the child's hearing – all these are sure to prolong the situation. If the grown-ups stop worrying, in 99 per cent of cases the stage passes naturally. Grandparents should keep their cool and show the way by appearing not to notice the hesitations. After all, stuttering is basically evidence of an active mind.

Tantrums

There is nothing better calculated to make you wish you were invisible than being in charge of a two or three-year-old playing up in a supermarket or other public place. Running away, fighting you and crying with shrill, pent-up feeling or holding the breath until he or she falls down, alarmingly blue in the face: any of these may be part of it.

With Johnnie tantrums started almost as soon as he was really mobile. His new independence was both exciting and frightening. His heady feeling of power was in conflict with an anxious longing to be looked after, even babied. His mother found shopping trips were torture. Unless he had instant gratification – a bar of chocolate or a toy that had caught his eye – or there had been an attempt to make him wear, say, his scarf or his wellies, he would protest with his whole body.

Diane, his mother, who had been so proud of her fine, healthy young son, was at her wits' end. His father, called upon to take a hand, was equally unsuccessful. Firmness, threats, reasoning or even a sharp slap had no effect in cutting short a tantrum, nor in making another one less likely. Often the parents' struggles made matters worse. Onlookers were disapproving on two fronts:

'What a badly-behaved child – dreadfully spoilt.'

'Poor little mite, with awful, bullying parents like that.'

Johnnie's parents were neither bullies nor indulgers: just worried. The doctor was quite helpful. He checked Johnnie for any disorder such as earache, which could be upsetting him. Johnnie was clear of infection, so the GP suggested that his mother should try to avoid too long a gap between meals or snacks. Sometimes a low blood sugar sets off a tantrum. Getting overtired can also be a trigger . . . Otherwise the only consolation the doctor could offer was that Johnnie would grow out of this immature behaviour. Tantrums are so commonplace as to be normal in the eighteen months to three years range.

That information didn't help with knowing what to do when a tantrum is actually happening. When Johnnie went on a shopping trip with Diane's mother, the granny of the case, he was not so likely to have a full-blown tantrum. One reason was that she concentrated on talking to Johnnie, slowing down to look at interesting spectacles such as men making a hole in the road, and discussing with him what they were buying off the supermarket shelves and why. His task was to carry the carton, or whatever, a foot or two and to put it in the trolley. At the check-out, a crunch point, he was made important by holding Granny's umbrella or something else of hers while she paid the bill. Then he had to look after the strip of prices so that they could check what they had bought when they got home.

If Johnnie did start a tantrum, for instance over a tube of Smarties, his granny hugged him and, through the racket he was making, she told him that she loved him to bits and that she needed his help: he was so strong and clever. Of course, this method didn't work like a charm, but it made things no worse. Just in case the little chap had been tired or hungry, they would take a bus home – if he liked bus-rides – or stop for a drink and a bun in the town. Smarties were not included.

Toddlers' tantrums are a cry for reassurance. Sometimes, as stressed and busy adults, we can forget that a small child may be overwhelmed by the size and complexity of the world he must cope with. He or she needs a guide to hold his hand and talk him through it, just as we do with an adult in an unaccustomed situation of danger and stress.

The lovely thing is that when your toddler reaches four or five, you can explain almost anything to him, and tantrums, stuttering and other difficulties of this first adolescence begin to disappear.

Terrible Toddlers Summary

- Another baby
- What toddlers can do
- Spoiling
- Sleep problems
- Fussy eaters
- Stuttering
- Tantrums

Chapter 4
The School Years and Education

Fιve-years-old is a very special age. It is nearly grown-up. At five your grandchild can eat with a knife and fork, wash and dry his or her face and hands and dress and undress, more or less. She can draw proper houses and people with arms and legs and features on their faces, and colour inside the lines in her colouring books. Boys of this age definitely prefer masculine-type toys – trucks and construction sets – while little girls may be ambivalent. They may go for Barbie dolls and cooking equipment, but they are quite likely to ask Father Christmas for a train. Either way, most games at this age seem to use up all the floor space.

THE BEGINNING

The major event of this year is starting school. Five-years-old in the UK means school is a legal requirement. Play groups or nursery school may have come before, from two-and-a-half onwards, but real school is serious. Up till now your grandchild's life has been centred on home, and the adults in the family seem the cleverest and most powerful people in the world. That is all set to change. For years to come the main focus is school, and the dramatic discovery is made that there is someone who knows more than Mummy and Daddy and Granny put together – the teacher.

Ettie was five in July, which meant starting at St Michael's in September. Already she knew some of her letters and could count up to a million – she said. In fact, she couldn't really cope with more than ten, for instance when Granny asked, 'Pick ten daisies for me,' that was a hard task. Conversation-ally, Ettie was confident and fluent and she could sing the lyrics of the latest pop music.

She was longing to go to school. I think she envisaged herself growing six inches overnight, carrying a satchel with pencils and books in it, and wearing long socks. So she was completely unprepared for the tragedy on the day. Mummy had taken her to school but Granny was going to collect her at 3.15. It was a bedraggled little soul who stumbled across the playground with the others, her face tear-tracked and her socks in concertinas.

She had wet knickers, and the shame was almost more than she could bear – until Lydia, her granny, told her that the very same thing had happened to her on her first day at school. The cure was completed by a change of clothes and tea at Granny's with fingers of bread and butter and jam. Granny always did fingers, and milk at her place was coloured pink.

This was the start of Ettie's education: a vital phase in her life. She would never be more receptive and responsive to new knowledge than now. Most children feel important in themselves as they tackle such fundamental subjects as reading, writing and sums, and the extras like music and painting and swimming. There's also the fascination of being with the other children and comparing. It is interesting to find out what time other people go to bed, how much pocket money they get and if they wear a vest.

Ettie, who had been so full of herself, began to have doubts. At home she was always the best – out of one – but now she found that there were some children who did better than she did. It wasn't fair. For the first time she experienced the fear of failure. Lydia saw her quite often, on the afternoons when Ettie's mother was working. As well as going for a walk through the park, having tea and half-an-hour of TV, there was a little time that Lydia could use to help Ettie with school.

She had passed the stage of naming people and animals in picture books, but loved the stories. She didn't mind having the same one over and over, and with big print and a picture on the *facing page she found she could read more and more of the words. It must have been like this when the Rosetta stone gave archaeologists the key to deciphering the hieroglyphs. Ettie had the thrill of discovering for herself what the writer was conveying. Lydia was admiring, as Ettie explained to her the school method of reading. That is one of the tricky parts. Your grandchild may be taught by the look and say method, recognizing whole words on sight, or phonetically sounding out, like C − A − T. You will only cause muddle if you don't stick to the way the teacher does it, at this early stage.*

From seven onwards it is purely a matter of practice: you can help by listening and sharing. By about nine, most children can read fluently enough to use textbooks in the classroom and storybooks for pleasure. You can help with practice and praise if your particular grandchild has slipped behind. This can easily happen if he or she has missed a week or two through illness.

YOUR GRANDCHILD'S MOTHER

The start of schooling is a watershed in a mother's life, which does not always apply to fathers. Your daughter or daughter-in-law is bound to feel a pang at losing her 'baby' and gaining a schoolchild, even if she has been looking forward to a little freedom for herself. The relationship has suddenly altered: the most exciting events in the child's life are those that happen at school. Home just fills in the spaces. Whatever else, be especially nice to the mother and think up some pleasurable distraction at this point.

A particular problem with school is that it stops and starts for holidays, and also hands the child back to full-time home care in the case of illness. This is often how grandmothers get drawn in.

Josie's grandson, Billie, started school and his mother returned to work. She had been in one of those extended unpaid leave schemes. There had been a lot of changes in the last five years, and she was anxious not to have time off, especially at the outset. So it was an SOS for Josie when Billie had a tummy upset in the second week. Josie ran a craft shop and managed to get a friend to hold the fort.

Josie knew that the young couple needed the extra income from her daughter's work and she wanted to help. A one-off like this was manageable, but what would happen at half-term and in the school holidays? She did not want to be committed as a stand-in at every turn. This meant a serious heart-to-heart with Phyllie – her daughter. In the end, Phyllie made an arrangement, for money, with another mother at the school. She had two younger children at home, and agreed to take on Billie in the holidays. He was in the same class as her eldest.

This left the matter of illness. In the age range five to eight, most children are ill about six times a year. Employers don't care for it, but often there is no alternative to the mother's having time off. Josie didn't mind helping occasionally.

Sometimes it is a bonus to have the opportunity of 'borrowing' your grandchild after school and in the holidays, and experiencing again the stimulus of having a young child about the place. Besides, this is a delightful age.

The school run

It can be frustrating if you are caught up in this side-effect of education: getting the child safely to and from school. How many years it goes on depends on distance, roads to cross and age, and whether you have a car and no fixed commitment.

The school run can be deadly: through the rush-hour traffic in the morning and right in the middle of the afternoon, so that you can't do anything else. The ideal arrangement is when several mothers each take a turn, but this isn't always feasible. As a grandmother you are likely to be drawn in if your daughter or daughter-in-law has a job. If you do find yourself on a regular treadmill, at least it gives you a wonderful opportunity of getting to know your grandchild, and also to pick up any difficulties that have cropped up during the school day. Bullying, drugs or getting into trouble with the teacher, or just not understanding some of the work – any of these may come out on the way home, while they are still smarting. You may be able to help, or at least alert the parents.

CHOICES AND DECISIONS

These early years at school are precious, the very essence of childhood; but they lead into a time when far-reaching decisions must be made and acted upon. Once your grandchild has taken the first step over the school threshold there is no turning back. He is inescapably in the educational system, and choices must be made which affect the rest of his life: career, friends, values. Making the choices is a minefield for the relations between grandparents and parents.

There are three subjects that involve the maximum risk to family harmony: religion, politics and schools. Of the three, schools are the most sensitive of all, since individual opinions are held passionately – 'because it is so important for the child'.

Suzette's husband, Henry, was proud and delighted to have a grandson, even if they had called him a silly name like Roderic. He was determined that the boy should have the best possible education, and he was prepared to fund it. The snag was that, while Henry was convinced that going away to a boarding school was 'the only thing for a boy', his daughter and son-in-law disagreed with him. They were imbued with what Henry regarded as soft left ideals and wanted their son to share his formative years in the broad mix of a state comprehensive, with the prospect of further education later – if he should prove to be sufficiently academic. Feelings about Roddy's schooling – although he was only six – were so inflamed that the monthly Sunday lunch became unbearable.

Suzette was slowly getting Henry to accept that the decision was not up to them, as grandparents, when Roddy developed quite severe asthma. Neither the rough-and-tumble of a city comprehensive with 2000 pupils nor the spartan regime of boarding school seemed ideal in the new circumstances. The compromise was a private day school, when the time came, but even then Roddy's parents didn't want Henry to pay the fees 'for fear of the strings attached'.

Sometimes the parents long for their son or daughter to go to a particular school, which they cannot afford without help. In that case, help from the grandparents is accepted with every protestation of gratitude. But even so the younger couple need to feel that they are in control.

For most of us it is more a matter of finding out what is available locally in the state system, and weighing up which school is likely to suit the particular child best. It is risky for grandmothers or grandfathers to put forward strong preferences but no one objects to going through the criteria for a 'good' school.

Features to look out for:

- a mix of pupils with enough bright ones to keep the teachers on their toes
- teaching staff and administrators both having definite academic goals for the school
- clear structure to the learning programme
- homework set regularly and marked promptly
- discipline and praise in the classroom
- size: preferably not enormous
- children given responsibilities early
- leadership among the children encouraged
- special interests: you may want a school which is especially strong on science, music, drama or sport because of the child's particular bent
- most of all it is atmosphere that counts. You feel it as soon as you enter: hopefully a sense of youth happily sharing the important task of mastering school subjects and enjoying sport and a range of extra activities

Plans made ahead don't always work out, but it is sensible to know in advance what sort of secondary school, or even which one in particular, the child and parents are aiming for – backed up by you. If the hope is for a school with a good record for GCSE and A level results, the years nine to eleven are key. Even if the main point in schooling is regarded as keeping the youngster occupied for a large part of the day, and for him or her to have fun with friends, he will be happier if he feels that his school work is important and appreciated.

This is where you can make all the difference. It's a killer if you ask, almost accusingly: 'How are you getting on at school?' It is better to find out what he likes doing and which is the most horrible subject – and show how impressed and interested you are. You must do some homework yourself, so that you know something about what he or she is learning. Then you can think of places to visit or things to do which have a bearing. 'Going to a museum' sounds totally boring but making a trip to see something special – place, picture or specimen – because *you* are interested, can make it a treasure hunt.

The summer holidays are an excellent time for such projects and these help to prevent the child getting out of touch with the school subjects. Often when children go back in September it takes them two or three weeks to pick up the threads they dropped in July.

May saw young Emma, nine-and-a-half, quite often in the holidays. Emma was finding her feet nowadays: she was aware of growing up and full of her own opinions. She definitely preferred her own sex – boys were stupid – and was one of a little group of girls who played and chattered together. One result of her increasing self-confidence was a propensity to be cheeky. May didn't react: she had found that this worked better than snapping back or painstakingly explaining why it wasn't very clever.

Emma was going to be a famous scientist or a farmer's wife: she hadn't quite decided. Either way it meant an interest in nature. May found that she had exactly the same interest in birds, beetles and wild flowers – and she had learned a little in advance. Walks with Emma became two naturalists exploring and discovering at every turn, with a bag of finds to take home. While it was high adventure to go somewhere special, the simplest weeds and commonplace garden birds provided riches in terms of wild life, once you really looked at them.

In winter and when it was wet, there were the museums. Nine-plus is the age when children can enjoy these. May and Emma didn't live in a big city but there was a particularly good, small local museum.

Sharing a special interest made the world of books, and even numbers, relevant – also selected TV programmes. Emma, like most children, enjoyed drawing and painting. Trees and flowers were good subjects and a trip with paints and paper for her and Granny gave an ordinary walk a new point. The two of them had an extra bond, a lot of pleasure – and some of Emma's school subjects had an indirect boost.

Nature has a fascination for most children and it is the gateway to science, but it can equally be granny territory if the favoured area is music, architecture or engineering. It only means doing a little finding out in advance. Up until the teenage years you shouldn't be left floundering because your grandchild knows more than you.

Eight to twelve is the age for theme parks, fairs and candy floss. On the whole these obvious treats are best left for the father and mother to provide – and get the kudos. Such gala trips are fun and children are delighted at the prospect, but there is nothing constructive about being whirled through the air until you feel sick.

If you have any talent for making things – recycling Christmas cards with glue and stiff paper, cooking jam tarts and birthday cakes, or making costumes for a play or ordinary, simple clothes – you have a head start as a grandparent. Most children love making things and it is fascinating for you both to share these activities while your grandchild still has not reached the age when they find out that grown-ups are often wrong. And hundreds of years out of date. 'Can you believe it – Gran doesn't even know how to use a mouse?' was the disparaging comment of a computer-literate young man of thirteen. His sister, two years older, remarked, 'Can you imagine the type of gear she wanted to buy me? Yuk!'

That stage, when you are assessed as shamefully ignorant, is to come. Something which is valued enormously at all ages and stages is your presence at sports days, school plays, carol concerts and prize-givings. Of course you have to look exactly right: that is, as much like the other mothers and grandmothers as possible. Pillar box red and dramatic styles are out – unless you are a well-known actress.

HOLIDAYS

Up to the age of around twelve, children, parents and grandparents often find it convenient and a money-saver to holiday together. It provides an added interest for the older generation, and for the parents the chance of some time on their own. For the children it means twice as many grown-ups to take them places.

It is wise to stay somewhere within striking distance of a town with shops and some entertainments to provide a change of scene, the chance of meals out and an escape in wet weather.

Before you plan a joint holiday you must be confident that there is no in-built hostility between any of the in-laws. Can you really face two weeks' close contact with your son-in-law or daughter-in-law – or vice versa?

The Examination Years

From thirteen or fourteen until the end of schooling your grandchild will be on a conveyor belt of studying for exams. Your role must be flexible.

> *Laura's parents were ambitious for her, and it showed. They were avid to know the results of every test and keenly interested in her homework. They insisted that she never went out midweek and that she had plenty of time for study at the weekend. Since Laura was conscientious by nature it meant that she played almost no sport, hardly saw her friends except in the classroom and in fact did nothing but schoolwork. The result was that although she did not do disastrously in the mocks, her marks were 'disappointing'. She was already stale, with three months before the real examination.*
>
> *The most helpful line her grandmother could take was to distract her from her studies, whether by asking for help over some practical problem in the house or garden or inviting her to something she could not resist.*

The first set of exams, GCSEs or their equivalent, usually cover a range of subjects. The A level group – usually three – focuses on a few subjects relevant to a university or other further education course, or a job: in fact to the teenager's whole future. Naturally enough, parents are likely to have definite ideas on which subjects are suitable, but young people have strong views of their own and these may be radically different.

Jeremy's father was a distinguished lawyer and his great-grandfather had been a judge. Jeremy was a good all-rounder and his parents expected him to choose those subjects which would form a basis for law studies. To his parents' dismay he told them that he would not mind doing English but that he was also choosing drama and music, since he intended to make the theatre his career. Drama school would be his first objective. Both the grandfathers felt that the law held far better prospects than 'hanging around hoping for work as an actor'.

His grandmother's task was to prevent a full-scale family bust-up. She could not appear to side with Jeremy but she could listen sympathetically to his viewpoint. She could also be sympathetic to the anxious parents. As she said to them, at sixteen Jeremy had so many years ahead that even if he insisted on taking the A level subjects of his choice, that did not mean that he could not change direction if he found acting the let-down his parents foresaw. That is one delightful advantage for youth – limitless time to try out and experiment while discovering their true metier. My adult children have nearly all changed their careers at some stage, without any dire consequences.

Teachers' advice on the subjects to take can be useful: it can also be biased. Every teacher worth his or her salt is convinced that their own subject is the best, and the charisma of the teacher may sway the child's choice.

Of course we want to encourage our grandchildren and give them confidence by saying how pretty their first, crude drawings are and letting them win at Ludo. That is for the junior school stage. When important decisions are being made a doting granny is a handicap. It is kinder to be realistic.

During this period of intense education the young teenager also has to grapple with profound bodily changes. The growth spurt may come early or late, with a dramatic effect on height – and status at school.

Alastair grew into a bean-pole, while Jacob was six inches shorter. They were both nearly sixteen. Alastair felt that he was always picked on because he stood out, and Jacob felt he was ignored. Sport is important at this level in school, especially team games. Popularity depends on how well a youngster plays. The tall ones usually do best. Another hormonal effect – but not growth hormone – is the awakening of sexuality. This too may develop much earlier in some than others, so that it is easy to feel different or inferior. All these problems are dealt with in Chapter 6, about adolescents, but they can impinge on school performance and make the difference between success and failure, happiness or despair.

Parents and other authorities have lost their standing as good and wise in teenage eyes: they are likely to be written off as hopelessly out of touch. You might think that grandmothers would be seen as even less capable of understanding. Not a bit of it. This is the period *par excellence* when grandmothers come into their own. Because you are slightly removed from both the family and the school, you have a clearer perspective on what is happening. More importantly your grandchild feels it is safe to talk to you. All that you need do is be ready to listen. Of course there is a tacit understanding, which you must honour, that whatever you are told, you won't pass on. The very special communication across the double generation gap is precious. Foster it by saying little and none of it critical. Reassurance is needed on three fronts:

- the unchangeable nature of your interest and affection
- the child's good and lovable qualities
- that whatever the problem, he or she does not have to tackle it alone: you are there to share it

The worries and upsets that may emerge through granny/grand-child confidences, as well as those you can see for yourself, are dealt with in Chapter 5, and particular aspects to do with adolescence in Chapter 6.

The School Years Summary

- Starting school
- Don't forget the real mother
- School run
- A good school
- Holidays
- Examinations

Chapter 5
Children's Problems

O NE BONUS of being a grandparent is being able to experience again – at secondhand – the wonder and joy that can fill a child to the brim, unmarred by adult cynicism. My granddaughter was fascinated by the marvels of natural history as she pressed her ear against the cat's fur to find where the purr came from, while my grandson was in transports of delight at the sight of the fairground. But there is a flip side.

Children feel their problems and hurts as intensely as their pleasures. It is as though the sun was suddenly switched off. Sometimes the cause may seem trivial to us, but the unhappiness is deeply felt. You can make it better. You are in a uniquely favourable position to see and to hear about your grandchild's problems in perspective. Added to that you have the wisdom of experience and basic commonsense, qualities that may seem thin on the ground in the generation one down: your children and their partners. Beware: suggestions and the kindest offers of help, unless you are asked for them specifically, are liable to be interpreted as meddlesome and interfering.

Eileen could see that Kim's trouble with her teacher and her lack of friends were due to her dreadfully bad manners. The other mothers did not want their children to pick up her language, and the situation could only get worse. Eileen believed that the root cause lay in lack of discipline, and was rash enough to hint as much – tactfully, she thought. Her daughter, Kim's mother, turned on her in fury: 'You always think you know best. You always interfere, and now you want

*to undermine everything I'm trying to do with my own child.'
Eileen's daughter felt that her own upbringing had been too
strict and she was determined that little Kim should be a free
spirit, able to say whatever she liked without the slightest
inhibition. Meanwhile, Kim was testing out the limits of adult
endurance.*

The ideal granny plays the waiting game. She has her own life and
interests and is not tempted to relive her younger period through
her children and grandchildren. Yet she must convey the sense
that her help and advice are always available – if they are needed.

FEARS AND ANXIETIES

Because they see and hear so much that they don't understand,
and experience so many things that they can't control, all children
are beset with fears and anxieties at times. You've only to see how
a tiny baby will cry in fright when there is a loud noise –
threatening, because he doesn't know what it means. Older
children, from twos to teens, have fears too, but usually these
are kept secret. This is partly because of the instinctive super-
stition that we all have: that if we put into words what we are most
afraid of, it will somehow bring it closer. Some adults shy away
from mentioning cancer, for example, as though the term itself
were contagious.

As always, as a grandmother, you are in a favourable position
for noticing when something is bothering your grandchild, and he
or she may find it easier to tell you about it than anyone else.
Grannies never say that they will go to the school and talk with the
teacher, nor can they stop someone's pocket money. Sometimes it
is the parents themselves who are the cause of a child's worries,
and then he or she certainly can't tell them.

*Brenda was five and had recently started school. It had a happy
atmosphere and her teacher, Mrs Bearsted, was a plump, cosy
woman whom no one could be afraid of. Brenda settled in well
and it wasn't until about six months later that she started
saying that she didn't want to go to school. She cried piteously*

all the way there, although Mrs Bearsted made a point of looking out for her and taking her under her wing when she arrived. Brenda's mother explained to her that everyone had to go to school, and asked if anyone had been horrid to her or what it was she didn't like. Brenda looked down and said there was nothing.

Shirley, who was Brenda's mother's mother, didn't ask any direct questions when she was alone with her little grand-daughter, but they talked in general about life and home and school and other people. Some of the children in Brenda's class came from broken homes. It was this which made it so frightening when she overheard the quarrel. It was about her father coming in late and not letting her mother know, so that the dinner was spoiled. Her mother had said in exasperation: 'Next time you do it I won't be here!' Brenda was thrown into a panic of anxiety that her mother would not be there when she came home from school.

Once the dreadful fear was out, Shirley and Brenda's mother could put it right.

Children have sharp ears and they easily misinterpret what grown-ups say. The fundamental fears of childhood are of not being loved and of being abandoned, but I have never heard a child who was able to express this openly. Often an observant granny can pick up the clues from her grandchild's behaviour. Again, you are in a better position than anyone else to make sense of the child's behaviour. You are far enough removed from the situation to see the whole picture, yet you have such an intimate relationship that you are trusted.

Among the small-sizers anxiety and upset can show in unexpected ways:

- tummy-aches and feeling sick: especially likely on Monday mornings when school is the trouble
- headaches: these are uncommon in children for physical reasons
- withdrawal: when a child goes quiet and doesn't want to

play with his friends he or she may have a physical illness, but an emotional upset is more probable

- eczema may break out or get worse when a child is under stress
- asthma responds similarly
- bed-wetting in a child who has been dry for years
- unruly behaviour

Michael had never been a saint. He was too full of life for that, but for several weeks he had been unbearably noisy and obstreperous. He answered back and banged doors and refused to pick his clothes up off the floor. His teacher, used as she was to difficult seven-year-olds, found her tolerance stretched to the limit. Everyone in his world was cross with Michael except his gran, who did not have to cope with his behaviour day in and day out. Besides, she had figured out that something must be worrying the boy: this wasn't like his usual self.

There was the move, of course. It wouldn't mean a change of school, but the family was moving into a larger house, just outside the town – partly because of the new baby who was on the way. Michael had a vague suspicion that perhaps he was being replaced by a new model – probably a girl – and he might be made redundant. This was a concept he knew all about – from his Dad's work problems. But the item that tipped the balance was the jokey remark his Uncle Bob had made when Michael was telling him about the new house: 'They're not going to take you along, are they? Probably leave you behind on the day.'

As he confided to Gran over a mug of hot chocolate, even if it was a joke, Uncle Bob's words kept coming back into his mind. He was, after all, a grown-up and might know something about his parents that Michael didn't. He didn't understand why he was being so naughty until he and Gran worked it out. Even if everyone was annoyed by his antics, at least there was no danger of their forgetting him. He couldn't get left behind by mistake.

Michael, like Brenda, was suffering from what the psychologists call 'separation anxiety'.

Irma had been clean and dry since she was three. It had been quite a struggle then but now she was ten, with such matters long forgotten. The bed-wetting seemed to come out of the blue: nothing unusual had happened at home, and at school she had lots of friends and was a form monitor. Her mother took her to the doctor, sure that there must be a physical cause, and he checked her out for a urinary infection. The tests were negative and Irma said that she wasn't worried about anything.

The sad part was that Irma felt so guilty and looked so miserable as morning after morning she found that her sheets were wet again. It was the guilt that gave Gladys, her grandmother, the clue. At about this time Irma's grandfather on the other side of the family had recently retired. He suddenly found himself with a lot of spare time on his hands. He did all the DIY jobs in his home and then at his son's house – Irma's father. He was often around and in fact became rather useful as a childsitter. Irma was delighted to have Granpy's company when her parents were out in the evening – at first. He called her 'my little sweetheart'.

Then she began to whinge whenever her parents planned an evening with their friends. They told her how selfish that was, and she looked guiltier than ever. A dreadful suspicion began to form in Gladys's mind, and the circumstances seemed to fit. Gentle talking encouraged little Irma to confess that she didn't like the way Granpy fondled her when they were alone in the house. She wasn't meant to tell . . . but Granny didn't count. The difficult part for Gladys was persuading Irma to tell her mother, since if she herself had said anything it might well have been put down to her nasty mind. In fact it worked out. Gladys lived too far away to baby-sit, but a seventeen-year-old student was glad to sit in and Irma's grandfather only came to the house when there was a family occasion and plenty of other people.

Jealousy

Jealousy between brothers and sisters has been a problem since Cain killed Abel. The arrival of a new baby is a commonplace event, one that is supposed to be happy. For a young child it is a major life-crisis, a threat to his security. The newcomer is set to steal some of the love and attention that had previously belonged to the older one. Some jealousy is inevitable, and it may show in different ways: nightmares of violent happenings, a flare-up of asthma or eczema, a run of destructiveness, or nail-biting – since biting the baby isn't allowed. Sometimes the pent-up feelings are expressed more openly with a suggestion that the baby could be 'sent back' or put in the dustbin.

> *Peter was two-and-a-half and without the eloquence and vocabulary to convey his hurt and distress at his mother's fussing over his little sister. He understood that he was meant to love her and often went over to the crib, saying 'Nice baba'. It wasn't obvious at first, but then his mother noticed that the baby cried whenever he had been near her. He had been quietly pinching her, under the guise of stroking or patting. Peter's mother was horrified and told Felicity – his granny. Felicity listened and pointed out that it was only that both little ones – Peter wasn't far out of babyhood – loved her and needed her so much. They worked out a plan together. Felicity offered to look after the baby for an hour or two on a regular basis so that Peter could have a special time with his mother, and sometimes Felicity took Peter off to spend time with her, away from the sight and sounds of the baby. As his granny pointed out, Peter was so big and sensible that he could play proper games and go to different places, not just lie there like his sister.*

Doing badly at school

Of course, there may be good, solid reasons for a child having difficulty with his lessons – deafness or Down's syndrome, for example. Much more often your grandchild started off at school perfectly satisfactorily and may even have been doing very well – and then, out of the blue, he or she begins falling behind and getting into the teacher's bad books. It can happen at any stage, and naturally enough the parents are worried. If your son or daughter is one of the parents you are likely to hear about it.

Celia's daughter, Nancy, told her the sad saga of young Rory. He had always been well up to average in his class, but now that he was coming up to GCSEs, and it mattered, he was scraping along near the bottom. This was especially noticeable in English. His father had read the riot act about homework and Rory had turned sulky and said that he was too tired. His work was even more full of mistakes.

Rory wasn't ill and his fatigue didn't extend to the football field or doing things with his friends. There had been no disasters in the family and although the school buildings were old, they were not unpleasant. The problems turned out to be with the teachers. There had been a run of supply teachers, each approaching the subject in a different way, then finally Mr Jones. Rory had annoyed Mr Jones from day one by asking some silly questions, and from then on Rory was the chief target for his sarcasm. Rory switched off: off the whole subject, off teachers in general, off schoolwork.

Celia was the one to whom Rory could explain: everyone else was too cross and anxious. Nancy was able to get matters right at the next parent–teacher evening when she discovered that Mr Jones shared Rory's passion for football.

Sometimes, when school isn't going well, Granny can make a difference to a young child's self-confidence by appreciating those talents he has:

Jimmy was never going to be an academic, and didn't have the heart to try. Everything went wrong for him anyway. About this time his granny discovered that he was a great help in the garden, though he was puzzled when she said he had green fingers because his radishes looked so healthy. He also had a way with animals, at any rate with Granny's cat Suki. When Suki was feeling poorly after an injection at the vet's, Jimmy was the one who managed to get her to start eating again.

These were only two of a list of talents Granny found to praise Jimmy for.

Lying and stealing

Lying

Young children, because of their lack of knowledge and experience, can say things which are very obviously untrue – to us. The three-year-old charmer with two older brothers was asked when she would be going to school. She answered confidently: 'When I'm a boy, of course'. As adults, and with the kindest motives, we take advantage of children's trust in us to tell them about Father Christmas or the tooth fairy. At the same time, we say that they must tell the truth.

My goddaughter, Charlotte, worried her mother by insisting that she owned a black horse. It was in her bedroom at present, but would gallop alongside the car when they went out – 'He always does'. This was harmless enough and could be put down to a vivid imagination, but her mother thought it was more serious when Charlotte insisted, just as passionately, that she had seen a bad man put the broken pieces of a porcelain vase behind her toybox. Sometimes it is the grandmother generation who have forgotten that for children up to age ten, at least, the truth is what you want it to be. Charlotte was nine-and-a-half.

It is vital in the training years not to corner a youngster into telling a lie. If you know a child has done something silly or wrong, say so – don't ask him if he knows anything about it, and then jump on him when he pretends innocence. The principle, right into teenage years, is that if you want the truth you must convey a cast-iron guarantee that whatever the child says you are not going to be angry. She or he has to feel safe to tell the truth, and because grandmothers have a reputation as softies, you are far more likely to hear what really happened than teachers or parents.

Stealing

This can often be worse than lying. For one thing, even a young child can get into trouble for taking other people's property or picking something up in a shop. I remember the dreadful humiliation at the check-out when the four-year-old who was 'helping' me do the shopping was seen to have a tube of mustard in her hand, which I hadn't noticed and didn't want.

While they may muddle up fact and fantasy, most children have a strong sense of ownership from about three, and they do realize that other people own things too. If your grandchild steals there is likely to be a definite reason. Sometimes it is a tangled-up form of generosity: a wish to give Mummy or someone else special a fitting present. It may not feel wrong to take something not for yourself but for another person.

The other type of stealing – for oneself – often has a sad basis. This is particularly the case when a child steals from his or her mother.

Julian was the Fosters' adopted son. As so often happens, the couple had the unhoped-for delight of having a natural son a few years later. Julian felt deprived of his mother's love and attention, and started taking money from her purse to buy himself sweets. He wasn't a criminal in the making, just a bewildered little boy who felt he had lost something of his mother and was trying to get it back. His grandma's warmth and reassurance helped him through a difficult phase, before he came to realize that a new brother could not take over his place. Adopted children are at especial risk of being judged with less indulgence than others: their parents always wonder what was in the genes their natural parents supplied.

With older teenagers who thieve deliberately from strangers and sometimes family members also, the problem is more serious. However much you may love them and want to help, this is too complex a task for granny therapy.

BULLYING

Nicola was fifteen: amazingly mature in some ways, but vulnerable. Her family put it down to teenage moodiness when she began shutting herself in her room for hours at a time, and misguided slimming when she only picked at her food. She was a clever girl and she was short-sighted. She had to use quite thick lenses and was helpless without her glasses. They called her Owly at school, but she said she didn't mind. She got on well with the teachers and had good marks, but she was hopeless at team games, so she had never been popular.

Barbara, her grandmother, lived 150 miles away and it had been six months since she had made the trip south to see Nicola's family. Because it was so long since she had seen her grand-daughter, Barbara noticed at once that something was dreadfully wrong and asked her daughter, Nicola's mother, what had happened. Once they were alerted, Nicola's mother and father found out what the trouble was. It had started in the September when Nicola had moved up into the GCSE class. This included some boys who had come from another school as well as a few new girls. A group of them had made Nicola the target for teasing and snatching off her glasses, and then frank bullying.

When Nicola's parents explained the situation to the school head she took the matter so seriously that the whole school was involved. In this case the bullying stopped, but sometimes there is no alternative to changing schools.

FRIENDS

All of us want to be liked and to have a special friend. This is especially important to your grandchild as soon as the home-centred years before age five are over and he or she has to hold his or her own in the big outside world, including school. Toddlers' playmates are just that: people to play with. But feelings don't run deep at this age except for Mummy and Daddy and, if you are lucky, Granny. It is from the start of school right into adulthood that friends matter so much. It is easy to take lightly the heartbreak of a young child when a best friend goes to another school, or their mothers don't get on.

Jenny and Jenny were firm friends. They had been in the same class at school since early days and on top of the coincidence of the same first name, they had a lot in common. They giggled at the same jokes and chattered together endlessly. They were roughly equal at games and both agreed that boys were horrible. Then Jenny B was given a place at a well-known grammar school while Jenny A was to go to the local comprehensive. Jenny B was thrilled and her parents were delighted. She was full of the uniform and sports equipment she must have. Jenny A knew she ought to be pleased for her friend, so she did not tell anyone what she felt. She wilted and moped silently.

Her granny understood. Grandmothers are often sensitive to the quieter pains of childhood that other adults may brush aside. Jenny A's grandmother felt it was worth spending time to find out what her granddaughter was sad about, and to hear all about her feeling of loss.

Lesser happenings can matter acutely to small people: when it rains on the day of a proposed birthday picnic, they can't go on a school trip because it costs too much, or a pet dies. The misery seeps through their whole being. Hugs and sympathy don't alter the situation but they help. The suffering may not last long but it is real – and it is cruel to say, 'Don't be so childish' to a child.

A consolation is that while a young child can be heartbroken at one time, at another he or she can also experience joy in a wholehearted way that most of us have forgotten. One of the privileges of being a grandparent is that we may share this: but we must never forget that it is to our own children, who have given us grandchildren, that we owe our best love and gratitude.

Children's Problems Summary

- Fears and anxieties
- Tummy aches and other nasties
- Jealousy
- Doing badly at school
- Lying and stealing
- Bullying

Chapter 6
Teenagers

Terrible teenagers, the despair of parents and teachers alike? But not of grandparents. This is where you win out. From thirteen to nineteen youngsters are trying to separate emotionally from their fathers and mothers, so as to prove that they are separate, unique individuals. Yet fiercely as they struggle to cast off the ties that bind them to their parents, they are apprehensive about standing on their own feet.

Grandparents are outside this internal/external conflict. In any language, Granny spells safety and being allowed to be a child still – without anyone knowing or any loss of dignity. Parents' instincts are wiser than they realize when they encourage teenagers to see their grandparents. It is scary, as a teenager, to be teetering on the edge of a world which the media tell us daily is full of danger and cruelty. It is frightening on a personal level, too, because of the fundamental changes affecting the youngster's own body and mind.

PHYSICAL CHANGES

Puberty comprises the developments that transform a child into someone capable of becoming a parent, and of running their own life among adults. It takes several years, longer in some than others. In general, it starts and finishes a year or so earlier in girls than boys. What makes it such a strange and confusing experience are the obvious sexual implications, unlike the ordinary growth in height and weight of childhood.

Changes in Girls

Girls may start to develop tiny breast buds as early as eight or nine, but it is from around eleven that the breasts become noticeable. Manufacturers co-operate in making garments to suit the girl who wants to feel grown-up but doesn't really need a bra. A granny is the perfect person for helping with this momentous purchase. The growth spurt, a period of strikingly rapid increase in height and change in figure, begins around this time. All the bones get longer, including those of the hands and feet, which means new shoes. The shape of the face loses its childish roundness to become more linear and chiselled: it gives an impression of heartbreaking vulnerability in the in-between stages. For girls, the peak age for growing is twelve, and usually it has petered out by sixteen. This can be a matter for regret, or a relief.

Another hormonal effect, not growth hormone in this case, is the awakening of sexuality. The first menstrual period is a major life-event for a girl. It can be a shock – even though she has been told all about it – an inconvenience and a cause of embarrassment and often of pain. It also invokes a fellow feeling, a sense of belonging with all the other women in the world since Eve. A granny is a woman who can understand, and knows about these things.

While the early periods may be a nuisance, it is usually after a year or two that many girls suffer period pains and occasionally sickness. Everyone knows that a healthy walk is good treatment for dysmenorrhoea, but there are times when a little 'grannying' is called for: sympathy, a hot water bottle, a warm drink and paracetamol. While the average age for starting periods is twelve-and-three-quarters today, some little girls begin theirs at nine, while others miss out until sixteen or seventeen: all part of the normal range. It is usually a case for reassurance, something we grannies are good at.

Changes in Boys

The timing of the growth spurt and its dramatic effect on height is immediately important in terms of a boy's status at school. The average start-up age is about twelve, peaking at fourteen and slowing towards a halt at eighteen – though some go on growing until they are twenty-one.

You are less likely to be involved with your young grandson's sexual development, but it is as well to be aware. Around twelve, boys begin to notice that their testicles are getting bigger and the skin darker. 'Wet dreams' come later, about thirteen or fourteen, a case for a discreet change of sheets if the boy is staying with you. At around the same age, his voice may crack and be acutely embarrassing for him, but at fifteen it is definitely deeper, towards manly, and the first fluff of a beard may begin to appear.

Although they seem so tall and full of life, teenagers are not nearly as strong physically as they appear. Their bodily mechanisms are unstable with such a rapidly changing structure to cope with. It is the tall, magnificently healthy-looking nineteen-year-old soldiers who faint on parade – not the veterans. Teenagers tend to vomit where a real adult's digestion could manage; their joints are easily dislocated, for instance playing rugby and they are more likely than older people suddenly to need glasses. Although the spirit is eager, teenagers are prone to fatigue – as though their battery had gone flat. This is one reason why this age group goes for stimulant drugs like Speed and Ecstasy.

Although they would be the last to admit it, teenagers need more sleep than younger children. At weekends, if they are allowed to sleep their sleep out, they may not surface until lunchtime. Bear this in mind if your adolescent grandchild stays with you. Boys usually need more sleep than girls.

Nourishment

Eating is a major interest in the 'teenage' years. Most eleven to thirteen-year-olds love food, although they may not have time to bother with breakfast. They usually go for chips, peas, baked beans, cake, ice-cream and, if they haven't caught the vegetarian bug, meat.

Despite a healthy appetite, girls may try to cut down the calories when they are fourteen or fifteen, but boys are still in the 'bottomless pit' stage. The twins, Michael and Martin, finished off two dozen jam tarts between them, immediately after a traditional Sunday lunch, while they stood in Gran's kitchen chatting. They truly hardly noticed what they were doing, and they weren't in the slightest bit plump. Between-meal snacks do no harm at this age unless a child is definitely podgy.

'I'm starving!' is a familiar phrase. Chunks of cheese, fruit, a sandwich, a chocolate bar or biscuits can all be useful to fill in the chinks. From your point of view, if you are entertaining adolescents, prepare as for a siege, but avoid anything they are not accustomed to. I remember a soufflé of which I was particularly proud – it had risen wonderfully well – being rejected out of hand.

With granddaughters of fourteen-plus it can be tricky. They may be into the slimming mode; this reaches a crescendo at the puppy-fat stage, about sixteen. There is always a conflict between naturally feeling hungry and the fashion, including what the other girls at school are doing. All you can do is to admire her hair or clothes, but never mention figure. Unless you are pencil-slim yourself, your granddaughter will assume that you are trying to make her your shape. Meals, including Sunday lunch, could be served on a help-yourself basis, with the choice to include lettuce leaves (no dressing) and fruit as well as the normal foods. Avoid any pressure 'just to try a little', any remarks about how much or how little she has eaten, or that 'it won't do you any harm just this once'.

Alice was sixteen. She had done well in GCSEs and was now studying hard for her A levels. She was also very pretty. Her mother was an attractive woman, but she could not suppress a few pangs of envy at her daughter's youth and freshness. It made her feel old and shopworn – all the more now that the marital relationship was sagging. Of course, she was proud of Alice, particularly her academic prowess, but Alice somehow picked up the message that growing up into a woman, rivalling her mother, was not what was wanted. Doing well at the exams would be popular.

In the event, the slimming craze swept through her form at grammar school and Alice found that she could do this, too, better than any of the others. Her weight – she had been quite sturdy – slipped down in a gratifying way to her target and past it. She also took to long, solitary walks and stopped seeing her friends. Dora, her mother, began to get worried and tried to enrol her husband Sam's support. Like many other middle-class husbands, his interests were centred on his profession. He believed that the only contribution he need make to the family was as provider.

Dora and Alice were on a collision course, with mealtimes the battlefield. Both were upset. Alice's grandmother was shocked to see how much weight she had lost, and guessed that this was anorexia nervosa, the dreaded starvation disease. She told Alice and Dora what she thought and managed to persuade them that Alice should see their GP. Alice was referred to a specialist, who felt that she would do better away from home to start with, since she and her mother were getting on so badly. The tension was harmful.

Granny's offer that Alice could stay with her for a month was a far more acceptable option than hospital. Alice agreed. In the more relaxed granny atmosphere Alice was able to respond to the therapy, and with many stops and starts regained most of her weight. For that she had to eat plenty of simple carbohydrate foods with her meals, and Build-Up between. Meanwhile, she and her mother were helped to develop a different, more adult relationship with a boost to Alice's self-confidence.

Grandsons hardly ever become anorexic, but if they do it means that there are dire problems in the family. It may be the run-up to a resentment-laden divorce with the child used as a pawn by both sides. In these circumstances your steadfast affection is doubly needed.

Bulimia nervosa, the eating disorder in which the sufferer has enormous, secret binges of carbohydrate food and then tries to get rid of it by making herself sick, can also crop up in an adolescent granddaughter. More often, however, it comes on in older girls, after they have left home, and it is usually connected with disillusionment with a husband or boyfriend. Of course your support would be valuable, if you knew about the problem.

FEELINGS AND BEHAVIOUR

You may have worries. Your teenage grandchild has them too. Twelve and thirteen-year-olds are concerned about school and especially their friends there, burglars and whether their mothers will always be alive and available. They may still be afraid of such animals as bulls and snakes, being alone in the dark, and big crowds. Anxieties about their appearance become increasingly important, especially for girls, and 'making a good impression' with their peers. School work and marks matter more, now that examinations loom on the horizon.

As well as worrying about their health, which is unexpectedly common, and how well-liked they are, the older adolescents take on all the troubles of the world – personally. They can be passionately concerned about the rainforests, elephants, global warming or pollution. Pollution may suddenly matter: in 99 per cent their views are radically opposed to their parents'.

Although they seem to chatter a lot, adolescents may not come right out and tell you when they are really worried. You have to read the signs and make it easy for them to talk, since talking is the best way we know of relieving anxiety. The younger teenagers show their tension in tummy aches and headaches, jiggling their knees if they sit down for five minutes, and silly giggling. Older ones bite their nails, pick their spots or twiddle a strand of hair – even to the point of causing a small bald area. At fifteen or sixteen they may be moody or grumpy, but they are much more able to express themselves verbally. Your part is listening. Grannies are famously good listeners and never cut you short or criticize halfway through.

SEX

Of course, worries to do with sex affect children who are growing up: will she ever have a boyfriend? Will he do it properly? Could he possibly be gay? You may feel out of your depth – that things are so different nowadays. You need not. There's a rumour around that boys and girls today are having sex when they are twelve and in serious danger of becoming pregnant by thirteen. While this may apply to a minority, it is a tiny minority and serious interest in the opposite sex doesn't usually start until fifteen.

What is the norm earlier are intense same-sex friendships or a crush on a sports or entertainment star, or sometimes a teacher. They may go out in a group or with someone of the opposite sex at this age 'just for something to do'. By fifteen or sixteen most girls have a boyfriend, usually a year or two older, but only half the boys do. You may find yourself the recipient of confidences that children of fourteen upwards find notoriously difficult to discuss with their parents. This can put you in an awkward position. Teenage confidences are sacred, yet there are some things you feel that the parents should know about.

Patty was in a major pickle: she was almost certain that she was pregnant and the boy, also just seventeen, didn't want to know. If the pregnancy was confirmed, Patty had vital decisions to make: about arranging a termination or some feasible way of keeping the baby.

Pippa's boyfriend was on drugs, not just cannabis but a cocktail of uppers and downers, including crack cocaine. He was amusing and lively and Pippa was fascinated by his exciting lifestyle. He was several years older than Pippa and she knew that her parents wouldn't approve, on that score alone. So she always told them that she was spending the evening with her friend Stephanie – revising. Pippa had only smoked a little pot herself.

When a trusted granny comes to know the situation in cases like these, what she has to do is clear – but dreadfully difficult. Somehow she must persuade the youngster to tell his or her parents, while offering sympathy and support throughout. It may be possible to forewarn the parents in general terms in advance and soften their reaction.

CIGARETTES, ALCOHOL AND OTHER DRUGS

Your grandchild is almost certain to experiment, at least with the first two. Whatever you feel, it is better not to be too condemnatory so that you don't lose your privileged position as a grown-up who will understand and who can be relied upon not to tell tales behind someone's back. On the other hand, you should convey that in your view smoking is silly, considering the health risks, and rather an immature habit. This can be difficult if the parents are smokers, but any bad habit is safer if it is in the open.

Similarly with alcohol: if one or both parents are heavy drinkers there is an enormously increased likelihood that your grandchild will follow. The snag, apart from health, is the damage done to school work at this crucial teenage stage in education. Lager in the lunch break makes the afternoon's lessons so much a waste of time – this argument sometimes reaches its target. As with adults, some adolescents drink to dull their sorrows – for instance failure in an examination, rejection by a friend of either sex or just not being popular.

The Good Angel aspect of being a grandmother may come into play in these circumstances. If you can enable the young sufferer to unburden to you what seems a hopeless tragedy, the mere act of sharing it will remove some of the sting. As adults, it is important that we don't make alcohol seem to be the answer when something has gone wrong by saying ourselves, 'I could do with a drink'. Nor should it come over as a particularly grown-up treat, any more than, say, coffee.

Glue-sniffing is an exclusively juvenile drug addiction, deadly dangerous and done in secret. The tell-tale signs are soreness round the nose and mouth, and at times a faraway look, loss of concentration and slurred speech. In between times the teenager is likely to be unusually irritable or moody. Glue-sniffing can run through a school like an epidemic – and then die out until another set is affected. Luckily most children give up the practice before it has done them any harm, but you cannot rely on this.

The usual reasons for trying it are 'for something to do' and pressure from a group of friends. Boredom is always dangerous for a teenager, and if you are able to add an extra interest into your grandchild's life and a sense that he or she is someone who matters, you may be saving him or her from dangerous experiments, not only with glue and other solvents, but with other more addictive drugs later.

MISSING DADS

You are needed more than ever by the child of a single-parent family. Nine times out of ten it is the father who is absent, whether by divorce, desertion or death. It usually involves the remaining family in the added discomfort of a reduction in income, although not in Jessica's case.

Jessica's father had been killed in a road crash when she was ten. Although she had been very fond of him, she had long since got over the mourning phase. Nevertheless, the longer term effects of not having a father began to show when she was seventeen. She was short of self-confidence, especially with boys. Her mother and grandmother gave her plenty of love, but she needed some male input.

It was indirectly that Granny helped most: by getting her stick-in-the-mud husband to take his grandparental duties seriously. In fact, he enjoyed being brought into everything and particularly taking Jessica to concerts. The other ploy was for everyone to take an interest in Jessica's tennis, including arranging some extra coaching, so that she spent more time at the club, in mixed company.

STROPPINESS

'What's got into him?' Awkward and truculent teenagers are commonplace: your grandchild may be one of them. A mild degree of strop is merely the way a youngster may emphasize that he is no longer a child, to be told what to do; but it may be so bad that you cringe at the rudeness he shows to his parents in particular, but visitors also. Yet you know he can be absolutely charming at other times. If you are to react in the most helpful way, you have to work out why the teenager is acting up like this. There is a range of possibilities.

Spencer Johnston had been an easy-going, obliging child, popular at school. Now that he was fifteen, just when GCSEs and A levels were looming, he had changed into an argumen-tative, unco-operative, moody youngster. If his parents asked him to do anything, that was the signal to say: 'Why should I?' and slam out. He had begun skiving off school with a group of other boys.

His parents were busy professional people: Winston, a solicitor, and Olivia, a primary school teacher, and they were both involved with local politics. Time was at a premium. They had assumed that Spencer would follow in his father's footsteps and study law. That meant concentrating on his homework over the next few years and not wasting his time at discos and the like in the evenings and weekends. They knew that it was particularly important for a black lad that he should have no blots on his reputation. Anyway, the Johnstons were a proud British family. The grandparents had come over from Jamaica in the '40s, and one set had gone back there in their retirement. The other grandmother, Eusebia, was a widow and lived quite near the Johnstons.

The atmosphere between Spencer and his parents was strained and resentful – both ways. Winston and Olivia were absorbed in their careers and had neither time nor patience with Spencer's shenanigans. They tightened the rules. Spencer flouted them and was rude into the bargain.

Eusebia was a warm-hearted woman, recently retired from a clerical job. She was always glad to see Spencer and watch him eat a huge chunk of her gingerbread. And they could talk without one eye on the clock. Spencer felt better because Gran didn't fuss if he was in a bit of a mood, and she, for her part, found out that Spencer had got the idea that his parents saw him as 'nothing but a nuisance'. They'd said so, and he believed them.

Eusebia knew that her son, and Olivia too, loved Spencer and only wanted the best for him, but they hadn't realized that a teenager needs more from his parents than a good home and education. She managed with immense diplomacy to explain Spencer's feeling of rejection. Like her they would need to praise him whenever possible, listen to his opinions with interest, and react with compassion when he was awkward and rude.

SPOILING

This is an especial temptation for grandparents. The arguments run like this: 'But it gives me so much pleasure,' 'You can't take it with you so why not give a little happiness now?' 'I only want to help,' or 'She's got a right to expect her granny to spoil her, it's only natural.'

Generous and loving grandparents who provide treats of all sizes can upset the delicate relationship they have with their own child and his or her partner. It is hurtful to outdo the rightful parents in giving their child pleasure, and difficult for them to accept happily even educational donations which by-pass what they could afford. All parents want to be the top people in their child's world: that is what having children is about. As a grandparent you have a unique and precious place as a source of good sense, affection and support to all the family.

Teenagers sometimes get into terrible financial tangles and may turn to you. Should you bail them out? As a one off, and with the parents' full knowledge and agreement – maybe. If you are generous to your grandchild behind the backs of his parents you are providing a dangerous lesson: that deception pays. For your part, don't be a soft touch, however much you want to.

Adolescence and the Law

It is a mix of good and bad, being eligible or liable.

Age 10   Responsibility for his or her own criminal actions, if he knew that what he was doing was wrong.

13   Allowed to take a paid weekend job.

14   Full responsibility for criminal actions.

16   May leave school and work full-time.
May marry with parental consent.
May consent to sexual intercourse.
May buy cigarettes.
May buy and drink alcohol with a meal only.
May consent to medical treatment: or refuse.
May ride a motor-bike.
Boys may join the Services.

17   Can hold a driving licence.
Girls may join the Services.

18   May vote.
May marry.
May be called on for jury service.
Can sign cheques, hold credit cards, have a mortgage, make a hire purchase.
Can buy and drink alcohol in a pub.
Can bet in a betting shop.
Can consent to homosexual intercourse – boys.

21   May adopt a child.
May stand for Parliament.
May hold an HGV or PSV licence.

Teenagers Summary

- Girls at puberty
- Boys at puberty
- What they should eat
- Anorexia and bulimia
- Emotional issues
- Stroppy teenagers
- The law

Chapter 7
Family Breakdown

O<small>NCE YOU</small> thought it would be easy when they were out of nappies. Of course, you soon found that you were wrong – but surely, when they have grown up, left home and married or made some other modern linkage, your work in terms of child-care must be over. Not a bit of it. With divorce as common as a cold in the head – affecting at least one in three marriages – your most difficult problems as a parent may be still to come. Only now you have the added complication of being a grandparent too.

BEFORE IT HAPPENS
Marriages and partnerships don't collapse overnight. Even if the couple have been trying to keep up a normal front, especially for you, you will probably have noticed some worrying signs. Your grandchild, who lives with them and depends on them for everything important in life, will be caught up in the tensions and unspoken words apart from any open bickering, when that breaks out. Their security is undermined. They dare not ask what is going on, and if they do they will be shut up and told not to be silly. So – they will try to work it out for themselves.

Any child of school age will have heard about divorce and know others who have only one parent left, or are shuttled from one to the other at weekends. Either way, such children could have lost their faith in the family as a safe, permanent base, a home with both parents together. From five-plus, your grandchild is aware of the dangers to dread.

Younger children may not understand about divorce, but the less verbal understanding they have, the greater their sensitivity to atmosphere, the emotions of their parents the tones of voice if not the words. They become confused and apprehensive of something unknown. This may show itself in several ways:

- clinging to Mummy and whingeing if she moves away
- a relapse into bed-wetting
- 'not feeling hungry'
- tummy pains, or odd pains anywhere
- scratching (making eczema worse) or nail-biting
- being generally awkward

For older children there may be a fall-off in their school work, so that they have the teacher's displeasure to deal with, on top of everything else. Also, because they are old enough to understand, they are now more at risk of being made pawns in the manoeuvring between their parents.

Even if a troubled marriage doesn't end in divorce, as well as the day-to-day unhappiness there is long-term damage to the child. Children whose parents don't get on are liable to have difficulties in relating to the opposite sex as they grow up. They may develop a deep distrust of marriage or commitment and, if they do marry, they are almost programmed for failure. *Your role* in this wretched scenario is important for your grandchild. You must be an unfailing source of calm, unchanging affection, and your home a haven. It is only natural that you should want to support your own child, either the father or the mother, but this is tricky.

As far as your grandchild is concerned, you cannot be seen to take sides – even if your daughter's husband is an utter swine or your daughter-in-law is an irresponsible spendthrift. Your grandchild is an exact 50:50 genetic mix of both parents. You cannot denigrate one of them without condemning half his make-up and heredity. Your attitude must be tolerance and kindness towards everyone – particularly if there is a possibility that a grandchild may overhear.

Molly's son-in-law drank too much and Julie, his wife, was increasingly angry and frustrated by his behaviour. Of course

87

Molly sympathized with Julie, but her heart went out to Dinah, a lively five-year-old who had recently become whiny and clinging. Molly made a point of avoiding discussion of Dinah's father's failings except when Dinah was at school. Otherwise, if the subject was forced on her, she murmured vaguely about the stress of modern living and the like.

If Molly had harboured any hope that she might act as a peacemaker, she quickly abandoned it. As a mother-in-law to one of the couple, she knew she would be seen as interfering or even blamed as mischief-making, whatever she said on the subject. So long as she didn't get caught up in the conflict, Molly could do a lot for Dinah. She reassured her that even if they were going through a grown-ups' rough patch, both her parents loved her as much as ever. And so did she: her walls were bright with paintings that Dinah had done at school – visible proof of her appreciation of the little girl and her great value.

AFTER THE BREAK-UP

It is easy to see parents who separate as selfishly harming their children. It is quite true that the children of divorced and separated parents are hurt and lose the carefreeness that should be part of childhood. The recent changes introduced by the government to make divorce blame-free and to provide mediation for each couple may help – a little. But there will still be those who split up and perhaps find freedom or relief for themselves, but not for their child. The main problem for him is the disintegration of his world and the major loss, at least on a day-to-day basis, of one or other parent, half his family.

However, there is evidence that living in an unhappy, quarrelling atmosphere is almost as destructive as divorce. Recriminations have no place. To keep your privileged position as a granny, welcome wherever your grandchild lives, may be particularly difficult if it is your daughter-in-law who is left alone to bring him up. If you have been obviously partisan in the past, you may find yourself excluded from contact with your grandchild. Despite the recognition of grandparents' roles in the Children Act (see p. 5), in practice there is very little you can do if your daughter-in-law or son-in-law refuses to have anything to do with you. The other grandparents may encourage this, in mistaken loyalty to their child. For your part, keep cool and don't do anything to jeopardize any vestiges of goodwill.

Send a card on your son or daughter-in-law's birthday to keep a line of communication open and continue to be careful not to criticize him or her in your grandchild's hearing. Little people have long ears and are liable to repeat what you've said, loudly and clearly.

After the trauma of a divorce your own child needs your love and support. Often, in the case of a daughter facing a sharp drop in income and a child to bring up on her own, practical help may be invaluable. If you are in a position to help – living nearby, without too many other commitments, and, most importantly, you are sure that you would derive some enjoyment and satisfaction from hands-on involvement with your grandchild – make a considered offer. If it is only a sense of duty that drives you, or it would mean giving up some activity that you value, don't commit yourself. Being trapped in an arrangement that has become irksome can spoil your relationship with your child, whom you are trying to help – and indirectly reflect on your grandchild.

If you cannot do anything practical, or only very occasionally, remember that your good-humoured interest and sympathy are a healing balm that is well worth giving on its own. Of course, if you are a natural with children and have time and energy to spare, you can be pure gold to the little family.

Rose used to collect young Graham from nursery school and give him tea before his mother came home from her job. Graham had always got on well with his granny. For one thing she had never been part of the family tensions when his dad lived at home. Signs of favouritism began to creep in – complaining when it was time for Granny to go home and even saying that he liked it better when she was looking after him. Rose could see that this was hurting Graham's mother's feelings, and might make her gratitude turn into resentment.

Rose reminded herself to talk to Graham often about his mummy: how good and clever she was, and how lovely it would be to give her a big hug when she came in. If they saw a robin on the walk home, that would be something nice to tell Mummy, and the picture he had crayoned would be a present for her.

The crunch for the child

Even with the most civilized divorce everyone suffers. Children react differently according to their age, their temperament and their parents' attitudes. In almost all children there is a period of mourning for the father or mother they have – to all intents and purposes – lost. As with an adult's bereavement, but even more acutely, the child feels guilty. If he or she had been really good the parent who has left would never have wanted to go away.

Alison and Lisbeth were fifteen and ten respectively when their parents split up. Christopher and his wife, Lucinda, had fallen out of love years before he met Patrice, but he was cast as the villain since he moved in with her after the separation. Lisbeth, in a way that is typical at her age, was fiercely supportive of her mother and left horrible messages on her father's answerphone. She refused to meet Patrice, so she did not see her father, yet inside she was torn apart.

The one person to whom she could admit how she longed to be friends with her father again was her granny, her mother's mother. The relief of saying it was useful in itself, and it was useful for her grandmother to know how she felt. Lisbeth's mother had been gratified by her younger daughter's 'loyalty' and tacitly encouraged her to believe that her father was all bad. Alison, Lisbeth's older sister, never joined in this mulling over her father's misdeeds with her mother, and had never wanted to break off her happy father–daughter relationship.

She soon arranged, off her own bat, to see her father. Lucinda was not too pleased, but at Alison's age no one could say that she wasn't old enough to understand and to know her own mind. It was through Alison and her granny that

Lucinda gradually softened her attitude towards the two girls seeing their father. Granny's flat was sometimes their meeting place.

Brian took on the role of looking after his father. Tom – his dad – had never been an effective character, although he was gentle and creative. When his wife left – she had offered to take Brian with her – Tom went to pieces. Brian, then twelve, took on the cooking, shopping and cleaning: this left him skimping on his homework and with even less time for fun with his friends. He was taking on adult responsibilities before he was even into puberty.

Only with his grandparents could he still be a child. Tom's parents put their energies into helping their son see what was happening to Brian and to make better practical arrangements for running his life and home. Granny, on Brian's mother's side, provided light-hearted loving care and a cascade of fun things to do. Some of them included Tom, whose own spirits revived slowly.

Some children simply grow up faster in reaction to their parents' break-up, without taking on the burden of an inadequate, or unintentionally selfish, mother or father. In fact they tend to cut off from grown-ups in general. It is a little sad that they should lose out on being young.

Other children go into reverse and slip back into the behaviour of a younger age – as though they could put the clock back to the time before their parents had even thought of divorce. Johnnie's relapse into bedwetting was an obvious example, at the mature age of nine. More often it is in a subtle loss of independence, not wanting to go anywhere on his own, anywhere new, or to take part in a school project, that the regression shows itself. Acceptance of the babyish behaviour must be the first response, rather than impatient pressure 'not to be so silly – you'll enjoy it when you get there'. As a granny, you must be the trend-setter. Fortunately, everyone expects grannies to be softhearted.

The next steps, aimed at strengthening his trust and self-confidence, include reassurance that what is left of his family, including you, are still there to guide and care for him. And that of course the absent parent loves as much as ever, even if they cannot see each other so often. The bricks of confidence-building consist of items of praise and admiration for anything the child has done which shows any hint of maturity or responsibility. Failures? Don't even notice them. Depending on the family closest to your grandchild, the recovery may take a few or many months.

Gilly and Peter reacted to the break-up in two quite different fashions. Gilly went quiet. She was thirteen, already in the throes of early puberty and her first periods – and their implication that she was on the way to becoming a woman. Like her mother. Gilly simply withdrew from the rest of the family and from her friends at school. She nursed her hurt and confusion in secret, in her room. Because it had been arranged, she saw her father regularly, but accepted their time together like an automaton. Both parents thought Gilly was sulky and almost gave up trying to jolly her along.

The one person to whom Gilly would speak – if they were alone – was her mother's mother. She was an active business-woman with a reputation for being nice to work for. She assessed the situation and set about melting Gilly's frozen heart and mind on her visits. It was her influence which enabled Gilly and her mother, and to a certain extent her father, to communicate the essentials – their feelings and fears.

Peter, Gilly's brother of fifteen, might have come from another planet. He was active trouble in contrast to Gilly's hidden unhappiness. He missed his dad, including the mild discipline which he could accept from a man but rebelled against when it came from his mother. He wouldn't get up in the mornings and stayed out all hours in the evenings, without saying where he would be. He began to smoke and from the sweetish, herbal aroma it was clear that he was dabbling in cannabis – and what else? His schoolwork went downhill, predictably, but remonstrations from his teachers did not get through.

Peter had always been fond of his gran, and still went to see her from time to time. She could see the lost, frightened child under the swashbuckling and bravado. Talking to her daughter, who was hurt and prickly herself, was not easy. Anything like criticism was out. In the end she tried the sympathetic route – and indeed Peter's mother was having a difficult time with the boy, even if Gilly was speaking again. Gran suggested, diffidently, that perhaps it might help if Peter's mother discussed the situation with the school head, and asked about sessions with a psychologist. If the school arranged it, Peter would be more likely to agree.

In fact, both Peter and Gilly and their mother benefited in their different ways from the therapy sessions which included both individual and family meetings. Some long-running, unspoken issues surfaced and could be dealt with, if not resolved.

LATER DEVELOPMENTS

Usually there is nothing good about divorce or separation from your grandchild's point of view – unless one parent was, for instance, a violent alcoholic. For the parents it may be a longed-for escape, a second chance of a happy life. One common result is an attempt to turn back the clock and recapture some of the lost youthful time.

Georgie's mother, Jane, felt like a girl again. After all, she was only thirty-four. Why shouldn't she live to the full and try to make up for the twelve years of misery with Steve? Georgie was embarrassed by her mother's ever shorter skirts and more transparent tops. She didn't mind so much when her mother went out in the evening, since there was always someone to keep her company, sometimes Granny. But she hated it when her mother brought one of her new men-friends home.

Even within marriage, children find it unpalatable to think of their parents having a sex life. Teenagers, who are open-minded about everyone else, are positively prudish about their own mothers' and fathers' activities in bed – especially *extramarital. Georgie was ten: old enough to know about these matters but too young to understand the feelings that go with them. Her grandmother was reassuringly the same as ever, dressing as she always did, and just as interested in Georgie's affairs.*

She explained to Georgie that her mummy must be lonely without Daddy, and, like little girls, she needed friends of her own age. In fact, Granny was pleased that Mummy had found a friend and said what a help it would be if Georgie was nice to him.

Allan's mother was the opposite of Georgie's. When she found herself without a partner she collapsed in a heap emotionally. She seemed unable to pick herself up and often wept. She told Allan how miserable she was, how hopeless she felt and that she didn't know how she'd manage. Allan was eight, an age when the world is still quite a frightening place. The shock and stress of his father's leaving increased his insecurity.

Instead of having a strong, all-knowing adult to help him through it, he realized that his mother was as weak and vulnerable as he was. He felt panicky, then angry that the grown-ups had let him down. He enjoyed Saturdays with his father – it is easier to provide a fun day when it is only once a week – but they only made the time at home seem worse. There was no one he felt he could rely upon. A grandparent taking an active role might have helped both Allan and his mother as they drifted unhappily with no sense of direction. Unfortunately the granny on his mother's side was in New Zealand, and his father's mother 'didn't like to interfere' for fear of being rebuffed as a stereotype mother-in-law.

New parents

It stands to reason that after a divorce one or both parties are likely to link up with a new partner. Often the new love was the final precipitant to the divorce. Another woman in the mother's accustomed place, or another man asserting his rights in the home: either way, love and attention which belonged to the child may be siphoned off.

Tina's father's girlfriend, Jean, had a warm, friendly personality and wanted to make friends with Tina. She finally lost patience when Tina consistently went out of her way to undermine her and wreck the relationship with Tina's father. Tina demanded instant love — then rejected it as rudely as possible. Her father avoided taking sides so neither was happy, and her mother was jealous of Jean and this rubbed off onto Tina. Tina dreaded going home to the endless inquisition: had Jean said anything about Tina's mother? What exactly? How was she dressed? What did they do? What sort of meals did they have? Did they quarrel? And, especially, did they seem to have plenty of money?

The grandparents on both sides 'wanted the best for Tina' but they had hardly ever met and were pulling different ways. Each tended to see things from the point of view of their own child, while what was needed was co-operation. The breakthrough came when Tina was in hospital after acute appendicitis. By chance both grandmothers came to visit her on the same afternoon, bringing identical presents. They got talking. The upshot was that they could see Tina's piggy-in-the-middle situation — too much for a seven-year-old to manage. They decided together that they, at any rate, would stop taking sides and try to soothe the hurt feelings in a conciliatory way. The tension slackened and Tina was happier. She saw her grannies more often and did not have to be careful what she said to either of them. She has made peace with Jean.

Another complication for the children in a divorce may be the merging of two partial families, when both new partners already have one or more children. The children are expected to get on with each other, despite suddenly having to share their particular parent and being told what to do by someone strange. You, as a grandmother, can see the dynamics of such a family in action. Your grandchild is 90 per cent certain to feel at times that favouritism is shown to the step-parent's offspring, and that when they are horrid there is no one to turn to. You cannot intervene directly – the set-up is explosive – but you can help such tangled families by your calmness and love, and your scrupulous even-handedness to your own and the 'new' grandchildren.

You may think that your contribution is pathetically small when there are such major, complex problems: like trying to empty a bucket with a teaspoon. But love never goes to waste, and if your grandchild can be sure that you will always be pleased to see her or him, always interested in what she is doing, and always ready with sympathy when she is sad or in difficulties – you are giving her something beyond price.

THE LAW

If your grandchild's life is completely disastrous or even danger-ous, following some family break-up, and in addition he or she wants to live with you, the courts may uphold such an arrange-ment (see p. 5). This is rare, however, and only a very last resort – even supposing you are able to take on the responsibility. What can happen, informally, is a grandchild staying with you during a difficult period. This does not give you any rights and the parents can take the child away whenever they like.

Family Breakdown Summary

- Signs of impending break-up
- What you can do
- The split
- Effects on little children
- Reactions of older children
- New daddy, new mummy

Chapter 8

Grandfathers

ONE OF my earliest, most treasured childhood memories is of sitting on my grandfather's knee and feeling the scratchy tweed of his jacket on my cheek. He gave me a shiny silver shilling. I saw my granny much more frequently, and loved her, but nothing I did with her stands out in my mind as vividly as this episode.

When a granny tries to be helpful or makes a suggestion, there's an even chance that she'll be seen as out-of-date, interfering or 'trying to take over'. By contrast, the smallest sign of interest from a grandfather is valued highly. If he plays with his grandchild he is admired as 'so good with little ones', and anything he says is treated with respect. From a toddler's viewpoint, Grandfather seems unimaginably old (at fifty), important and an infallible source of knowledge on all subjects. The halo effect of grandfatherhood extends through all the later stages of childhood, into adolescence. Grandfathers are special. Mothers, grannies and aunts are just ordinary.

The chances are that you are married to a grandfather. To you he seems much like other men, incorrigibly human. However, since he has such a flying start in his relationship with your grandchild – and his – why not turn this to good account? Encourage your partner to be involved because he can exert such a beneficial influence as well as giving a great deal of pleasure. Games, trips and helping in the garden with a grandfather are all seen as treats, and conversations as a serious interchange of views.

POSITIVE EFFECTS

Stimulation of Interest in Worthwhile Subjects

These may be indirectly related to school work, like stories about the past; practical, like carpentry; or enriching, like music or nature.

> Cressida started her scientific career at four. Her grandfather showed her the magic of a magnifying glass, and at another time a magnet. One day they made handkerchief parachutes to carry small toys and Grandfather's pen safely down from an upstairs window. Physics is frequently a stumbling block for youngsters who want to study such subjects as medicine and engineering at university. Cressy knew the basic principles before she even started big school. When physics came up in the curriculum it held no fears for her.

Going to a football match with Grandad, who knows the finer points, can set off a lifelong passion for the game, or growing radishes in a grandfather's garden may be the beginning of a delight in gardening.

Giving Advice Without Giving Offence

Unless they ask for it, and usually they don't, children may not take kindly to advice from grown-ups – except occasionally when the grown-up is a grandfather. Due to his privileged status, suggestions from Grandpa are likely to be taken seriously. They may be about the best way to do some practical task like measuring wood, or about more important subjects such as careers. It can never be too early to mull over this subject and anyway it is enjoyable to think of what you'll be when you grow up.

From around eleven, children have to consider what subjects they want to study in greater depth when the examination choices come up. It is no good following the whim of the moment if it lands the youngster in the arts arena when she will need science for her future career. My daughter, who is a successful barrister, was inspired to follow this line by my stepfather – her grandfather. He was a lawyer and loved it. He could easily be induced to talk about knotty points of the law and cases which had made an impression on him. His pleasure was catching.

The principle would have been the same if he had been a master plumber, a doctor or a market gardener. Also, as well as his own profession, he knew about the rewards of other work, from the careers of his contemporaries, some of whom he had known since his grandchild's age. Schools careers information and vocational guidance firms make every prospect look grey, but a grandfather has solid experience of the working world as well as a personal interest in the grandchild generation.

Promotion of Good Manners

Grandfathers are sufficiently removed from the hurly-burly of family life to be treated with a degree of respect. The cheeky monkey that his parents may have to endure does not necessarily try the same tricks on his grandfather. For one thing, the older man probably wouldn't put up with it. The other aspect is that the over-forties, the grandfather age group, have themselves acquired enough self-assurance and worldly wisdom to show respect to other people – including children.

If small people are treated courteously they tend to respond in kind. They are wonderful mimics, as you find out when they repeat something outrageously tactless they've overheard. With parents, brothers and sisters, what they may copy is from family nature in the raw. Parents are operating under the two-way strain of running their home and coping with their jobs, complicated by the demands of their children. No wonder manners may slip.

Stephanie's 'little chats' with Grandad certainly helped her get a place at St John's. She particularly wanted to be there for her secondary education because that was where her best friend was going. Stephanie hadn't got any special points in her favour, such as having a sister at the school, so it depended on the impression she made on the Head and one of the governors at the interview. Stephanie's polite, sensible attitude and lack of diffidence in talking to older people had largely been acquired on the walks she took with Grandad on Sundays.

This useful experience will also stand Stephanie in good stead when she has to go to college or job interviews and to get on with new people whatever their age and culture.

Putting Moral Values Across

When the hormones of puberty are running, any time from age nine, children want to show that they are different from that generation of squares, their parents. They disparage their elders' taste in clothes, music and, most fundamentally, basic values. If a father or mother speaks of honesty, trust, fairness and being kind, the response is likely to be 'Yuk!' Anything the parents believe in is assumed to be out-dated and prejudiced and irrelevant to the young. Grandfather can get the message across without even trying: by reminiscing about the people he has known in his life, the goodies and baddies, and why some were such good friends.

Grandfather Dickens, his mother's dad, made Alex's eyes round with wonder when he told the boy about his experiences in the Falklands War. There was the time when he was wounded on a night raid, but could not make the slightest sound in case the enemy located their position. When Alex had to have his tonsils out and his throat hurt badly afterwards, he remembered his grandfather's story and didn't cry. The nurses said that this helped the other children in the ward not to be frightened. Alex explained that being brave ran in his family. He was six.

Most family traditions are good, and there is no one better than a grandfather to put them over, since he is often part of them. Learning self-control, as in Alex's case, is one of the hardest lessons.

STAND-IN FATHERING

There is no one as appropriate as a genuine grandfather to make up in part for a child's loss of a father, whether by death, defection or divorce. It may work out if the mother finds another partner, but often the new man does not welcome having to take on another man's offspring. He grudges the time and love his wife or partner lavishes on the child. A grandfather has no such hang-ups. His grandson or granddaughter is only one step down on the direct blood line, and he is glad to see the mother's affection for the child.

The term grandfather conjures the idea of a Father Christmas figure, old and venerable. In fact the grandfathers of younger children are probably in their late forties or fifties – well able to play energetic games and very much in touch with modern life. What they bring to the single-parent scenario is a model of male thinking and behaviour to complement the feminine approach of mother and grandmother. Boys brought up in an all-female family setting do sometimes have more feminine interests and attitudes than the average.

Those of either sex growing up without a dad are less confident than the norm in their relations with the opposite sex.

The chances are that the grandfather will be most useful when it is his daughter who is partnerless – but what if it is your son who has split from his wife or girlfriend and child? Of course, encourage him to maintain contact, but it is also important for you and your husband to try and stay involved, for your grand-child's sake.

MONEY MATTERS

It stands to reason that with a twenty or thirty years' start you and your husband are likely to be better off financially than your children. There is an inexorable rise in the cost of everything – clothes, toys, holidays, schools and daily living – which affects those with a young family worst of all. Added to that, today's sophisticated children want so many things that were unimagined a decade ago – just to be the same as their friends. Parents may find their budget frighteningly over-stretched, while they haven't even the reassurance of job security nowadays.

If it is in your power, should you offer to help? It may be a satisfying experience to be able to open doors of opportunity for your grandchild which would otherwise be shut. If yours is a family that has always placed education high on your agenda, it may well be that the grandfather in the case will be keen to enable the boy or girl to attend what is seen as the best available school. If he or she is at a state school there may still be considerable expenses to enable him or her to benefit to the full, for instance for school trips abroad or extras like music, ballet classes or tennis coaching.

A grandfather's offer to contribute may be accepted thankfully. Or not.

Financial dealings within a family, especially when it includes an in-law relationship, involve a high risk of hurt feelings, misinterpretations and crossed wires. The younger couple are bound to be on the defensive because they are judged to need help from their elders. You have to go out of your way to preserve their dignity. Gifts are simpler to handle than loans since there are fewer opportunities for problems later, but it is often better not to pay, for instance, the whole fee, but as substantial a proportion as is necessary. This way you can refer to it as 'just topping up'.

Any money the grandparents contribute should go, in the first instance, privately to the parents rather than direct to the school or whoever is to receive it ultimately. Naturally, it would be enjoyable to have a little credit from your grandchild for your practical expression of affection. Unfortunately it works better for family harmony if you insist that this is a private arrangement between adults and you don't want the child to know about it.

Apart from the sensibilities of the parents, you don't want your grandchild to feel under an obligation, and uneasy if he doesn't do well at whatever you have paid for. Worst of all is if the parents prompt the child to show some gratitude. That way lies tension and even resentment where there should be affection.

Another danger is 'strings' – you hope to impose some conditions or choices because you have paid. You may feel that you want to help the young family but that ballet classes are pointless, while buying a viola or funding a school ski-ing trip is worthwhile. Even more fundamentally, grandfathers often very much want their grandsons to follow in their footsteps – school, college, career or family firm or sport. Strings are a certain recipe for conflict, often between the two parents as well as between grandparent and parent. Be sure that when you and your partner make a generous offer, there are no hidden strings.

Even without money coming into it, it can be difficult when a grandfather holds strong views about his grandchild's future. They are usually less intense when a granddaughter is involved. Often grandparents want their grandchildren to live out for them the careers and experiences they feel that they missed out on themselves.

A final risk factor in being a grandfather, also often concerned with money, is favouritism. A grandfather may have a penchant for his pretty little granddaughter and want to load her with expensive presents, without bothering about the equivalent for her brother. More likely, however, it will be like the Robertson situation.

John Robertson, like his father and grandfather before him and his son after him, had been to a prestigious public school in the north. When his daughter-in-law provided him with a fine little grandson, John Peter, it more than made up for the twinges of disappointment he had felt when his two little granddaughters had arrived. Of course he was fond of them, but they were, after all, girls. The school was hideously expensive these days, but John was determined that, by hook or by crook, the run of Robertsons would not be interrupted. The money would be found, somehow.

He could sell some equities: it was well worth it. John unfolded his financial plan to his son and daughter-in-law and waited for their approbation. Glenda, his daughter-in-law, looked at him with steely eyes: 'And what about Laura and Felicity – where do you suggest they should go to school?' John pointed out that he couldn't afford to pay for private schools for all three grandchildren. The girls would probably prefer the local school anyway. Besides, they'd get married. The unfairness would have upset Glenda even if she had not been a feminist. As it was, she was furious.

John's son could see his father's point and discussed with Glenda whether they would be right to refuse such a generous offer. She was disgusted and the atmosphere between them was soured at a time when they had everything to feel happy about, with three healthy, perfect children.

The best of intentions can be the most dangerous if you are a grandfather or a grandmother.

Grandfathers Summary

- Grandfathers are special

- Benefits of having a grandfather

- Manners and moral values

- Grandfathers and money matters

Chapter 9
Ready-made

Y<small>OUR CHILDREN</small> and your grandchildren carry your genes in every cell of their bodies. It is something fundamental: the one guarantee of immortality, regardless of your religious beliefs. They will hand them on in turn to the next generation, in a relay race that never ends. You don't love your grandchild just because of this but it does give you a personal stake in everything that happens to her or him.

'You can see he's got the Robertson chin,' or 'Look – she's got her grandmother's eyes: I wonder if she'll be musical like her, too.'

You know the scene: everyone gazing down at the tiny being in the cot, trying to spot a likeness. One of the endearing, fascinating features of a newly born grandchild is his often absurd resemblance in miniature to some family member. Later on you have the pleasure and interest of tracing out talents and temperamental traits in your grandchild that you have met before in your children.

In the ordinary way you have plenty of advance notice of a grandchild on the way: happy months of planning and wondering and hoping – and some anxiety – before the great day. You may have knitted some tiny garment or accompanied the mother-to-be on a shopping expedition to Mothercare for maternity wear and baby gear. What if you miss out on this pleasurable build-up and time to adjust to the idea of being a granny, but instead a fully-fledged grandchild is wished upon you? There are several ways this can happen.

Veronica's daughter, Barbara, and her son-in-law, Theo, had been married for nearly eight years. At first they hadn't wanted children, but later when Barbara stopped the Pill, nothing happened. Nothing happened for five years and they were now both well into their thirties. They were told that Theo had a low sperm count and that Barbara's bout of PID – pelvic inflammatory disease – would have reduced her fertility too. In fact, the doctor said, their chances of achieving conception were negligible, and if they were hoping to adopt they should not delay. Younger parents get priority.

There hadn't been much time to sound out the grandparents-to-be when the couple were contacted by the local authority. They were lucky and snapped up the chance of a baby boy who had had a difficult birth. At first the side of his face was puckered and he couldn't properly open his left eye, but Barbara and Theo were assured that this would right itself, over the first few months. To Veronica this was the most unattractive baby she had ever seen, not at all the cherub she had envisaged as her first grandchild. Doug, her husband, was even more forthright and said that he would rather leave his money to a cats' home than to a child he knew nothing about.

There were arguments and recriminations on both sides, so that in the end the older and younger couples did not speak for nearly four months. Veronica's friends told her she was in the wrong and that she should make the first move towards making up. So she set out with apologies and some presents. Baby Simon favoured her with one of his wide, toothless smiles and she said, 'I'm your granny, little Simon'. She found it was, after all, possible to feel warm and protective to a grandchild who did not have a blood tie. Doug took a little longer to come round but by the time Simon could stand up on wobbly legs and had said his first real word he was beginning to take a grandfatherly interest.

If a natural child arrives to a couple who have previously adopted, the first child could easily learn to hate the interloper who is stealing the love and attention that had been theirs. Grandmothers, from whom limitless wisdom is required in such family situations, have to act as leaders. They at least must never say anything about the new baby without first praising the first child, and they must pull out every stop to reassure and boost his self-confidence.

It is too easy, too tempting, to be carried away on a wave of warmth and happiness into favouring the natural grandchild. But that way lies disaster, with unhappiness for both children. You can fall into a similar problem if you have two children, one who has had a child in the ordinary way and the other who has an adopted youngster or one from a partner's previous marriage. Although the effect of favouritism may not be obvious immediately, it is bound to come out eventually and then it will be your own child who will feel betrayed by you.

Sometimes you are presented with a special kind of grandchild or even two or three together after the turmoil of a divorce. These children are likely to be older and their reactions complicated by their parents' break-up, and the tension of the bonds they have already made. A child in this situation may shuttle back and forth at weekends and in the holidays, from one parent to the other – with an intensive debriefing session at either end. You will be involved in the grandparent role if your son or daughter links up with a divorcé(e) with one or more children.

When a child is caught in the middle of a war between divorced parents, a granny can be a blessing beyond price: if she is resolutely non-partisan, never talks to the child about her parents' affairs, but is consistently loving and interested in her. Of course this is not easy when the child in question belongs to the earlier marriage of your son's or daughter's present partner. There is no automatic flow of affection and protectiveness when you are faced with someone small but awkward, whose existence is likely to be troublesome for your child. More second marriages founder over problems with children of earlier partnerships than for any other reason. As a calm, supportive grandparent you may be able to reduce the risk.

A somewhat similar situation may arise when a mother or father dies, leaving a lone parent with the child or children. Complications occur for a new partner who takes on the now single parent.

You might think it would be easier without a divorce in the background and the parents both still around, but not so.

Honor was in her sixties when her daughter, Valerie, married Gordon. It had looked as though Valerie would never marry. She was the matron of a private hospital, well-paid and extremely well-thought-of. She was absorbed in her work. Honor was proud of her, but not entirely happy at the thought of Valerie being on her own for the long years after she retired. Valerie was forty when the relationship with Gordon started. Gordon was one of the consultants whose patients were treated in the hospital. He was about fifty and a widower. His wife had been killed in a car crash some years before, leaving him with three small children. Housekeepers and nannies had looked after them, but now they were past the stage for nannies: the boys were ten and twelve, and their sister Louisa was fourteen.

Honor encouraged Valerie to accept Gordon's proposal. As an only child, Valerie had no experience of youngsters but she was confident in her own managerial skills. The children were not easy: their lifestyle had left them dissatisfied and demanding. The boys were exhaustingly active and non-stop noisy, but Louisa was the major problem. She was angry with her father for his 'disloyalty' in remarrying and resented Valerie's presence. She was constantly rude and disobliging – and all the worse when she found she could provoke Valerie into losing her cool. Gordon tended to side with his daughter.

The prospect looked bleak. Honor wished that she had not influenced Valerie so wholeheartedly into getting married. Nevertheless Honor was the one person who might be able to help. Louisa, whose own grannies were both dead, was polite to her. This meant that they could have a proper conversation. The girl sorely missed having her mother, or in fact any older woman, to whom she could turn for advice or comfort. The situation had put her at odds with Valerie, but Honor after all was a mother, and her interest and warm concern gradually softened Louisa's protective shell.

Honor had always sympathized with Louisa's predicament

*and she was genuinely glad, in the end, that she could be a
granny to her. After all, this was the only granddaughter she
was ever likely to have, and together with the two boys it
opened up a huge range of new interests for her. It was largely
due to Honor's grannying that these three youngsters did not
get caught up in dabbling with drugs or any other of the
reckless behaviour that children slip into when they are short of
family support and feel that 'no one cares'. Of course their
father loved them and Valerie wanted to learn to do so, but they
could not see this for a long time.*

Now that fertility treatment is widely available – at a price – there is
the possibility of your having a grandchild whose father is
unknown, even to the mother. If a man is unlucky enough to be
unable to father a child, he and his wife may opt for AID: artificial
insemination by donor. The anonymous provider of the vital sperm
is sure to have been young, healthy and intelligent, for instance a
medical student. But there is no possibility of finding out any more.

An AID baby is just as closely related to you as any other
grandchild, if your daughter is the mother, but there is no actual
blood link if it is your daughter-in-law. There is always some
curiosity about what traits or talents inherited from the biological
father may come out. One such boy I know is now sixteen. It is
interesting that he is very keen to study medicine, although there
are no doctors in the family.

RULES FOR AVOIDING FAMILY ROWS AND SPLITS WITH A READY-MADE GRANDCHILD

It is natural and understandable for you to have reservations about
a grandchild who is not genetically related to you. That doesn't
mean that you aren't going to be perfectly kind and affectionate,
especially at the baby and toddler stages. Later, however, you may
not feel like being as generous as you would have been to your
own flesh and blood. What if the youngster starts behaving badly?
It is tempting to put it down to bad genes – but not from your
family – rather than, for instance, the strain of being a child with a
distorted home background.

Darren's mother, Anne, was a South Londoner through and through and his father was a handsome British Afro-Caribbean who wasn't cut out for fatherhood. The marriage collapsed soon after Darren was born, and in due course Anne's old boyfriend re-appeared on the scene. They'd been at school together and he was the man she should have married in the first place. Roy was quite willing to take on young Darren, a good-looking boy with pale brown skin, his mother's features and tight, curly hair. Roy's mother and father made a big effort and all went smoothly until Darren was nine.

He'd always been inclined to exaggerate – usually to do with how strong and clever he was. Then he started coming home from school with fantastic tales of the daring and heroic things he'd done, most of which were impossible. Anne and Roy remonstrated with him mildly, but his granny, Roy's mother, told Darren it was wicked to tell lies. As she said: 'It's better to put a stop to this nonsense straightaway, before it gets out of hand.' Darren didn't improve but tried to keep out of Granny's way. That's when the stealing began: little bits of money from his mother's purse, which she couldn't be sure about. Then it was larger sums, so there was no doubt. Worse was to come. Darren started stealing at school – other children's lunch money, or pencils and finally a watch. He was found out.

Anne was distraught and Roy was worried for her. His parents started talking about 'bad blood'. The Child Guidance therapist who was brought in told Anne and Roy that the lies and stealing were characteristic symptoms of insecurity, particularly an uncertainty about being loved and wanted. The answer was for the adults in his life to give Darren more obvious affection – that included his grandparents. The new approach didn't make things change overnight, but they improved over a month or six weeks. The attitude of the grown-ups had adjusted for good. Children who steal from their mothers are nearly always trying to get hold of more love.

Because of his appearance, Darren had probably been the subject of remarks, directly from other children, but more importantly, overheard from adult conversation. This had

*undermined his confidence: his behaviour was nothing to do
with his genes. It is worth remembering that the most well-
loved and highly valued natural heirs may behave just as badly
as genuinely deprived youngsters – but the tendency is to make
excuses for them.*

If you have a ready-made grandchild, say from your son's marriage,
and another whose parents are your daughter and son-in-law, it is
particularly difficult not to show a bias: similarly if you have an
adopted and a natural grandchild in the same family.

Four essential ploys:

1. Scrupulous fairness between all your grandchildren when it
   shows: for instance, equal-sized presents under the Christmas tree, or equal cash hand-outs at the fair.
2. Equal interest and fairness in private, when the children are
   not present but you are talking with their parents. You may be
   tempted to give more, and show more concern over the
   natural grandchild, through the parents. Quite without
   planning it, you notice something in the shops that you
   know would suit this child. You can't – or don't – resist getting
   it. The same doesn't happen for the ready-made grandchild,
   unless you make it do so. Bias and prejudice, however
   carefully you try to keep them under wraps, have a way of
   seeping out. Even if they are kept secret they sour the family
   atmosphere. Your child and partner must be able to believe
   that you value their particular child as highly as any other.
3. Matters of money: equivalent amounts for each child. It
   may be that one seems more deserving, or to need something special that you approve of. However well you reason
   it out to yourself and your partner, it will appear to be
   favouritism to one child and having a down on the other if
   you give more to either.
4. Your will should not leave a legacy of conflict. The only safe
   way is to be absolutely even-handed as far as your children
   and grandchildren are concerned. No one can criticize your
   memory for that, nor can anyone feel unfairly treated.

Why This Meticulous Fairness Matters So Much

The main reason for being obsessionally fair is that any deviation will harm not only the ready-made but the natural grandchild as well.

The favoured one may come to feel superior by right, and become selfish and spoilt. This won't make him or her popular in the real world. The disadvantaged grandchild may feel inferior or resentful – and give up trying to be good. Sometimes the child who is most upset by any unfairness is the one who is given more than his share of the goodies. He or she may feel very protective towards one who seems unlucky. Worst of all, signs of favouritism may teach both children to be greedy and self-seeking, competing with each other to see who can get the most from Granny or Grandpa.

The golden rule – from day one and always – is to behave lovingly towards any grandchild, from any origin. It is all the more important to be demonstratively affectionate when the child is rejecting and rude. Look upon it as a symptom and feel sympathy. Children have a built-in capacity to learn, and if you are consistently loving the child will learn to love you. It is a wonderful privilege to be loved and trusted by someone who is still in the age of innocence. He or she will love you just as much when you have a revolting cold, don't look as smart as the assembled company, or your cakes have come out like biscuits and the jelly won't set. Even if you were only 'doing the right thing' to start with, you won't be able to stop your own feelings from becoming genuine love.

Ready-made doesn't always work out, but at least you can make sure that any problem is not due to you as a grandparent. Children who are not living with their two natural parents and feel fed up in passing, or more seriously unhappy at home, may start thinking that their real, absent parent would be so much nicer than what they have. Curiosity may also come into it.

Kelly was the adored adopted daughter of the Henfields. At fifteen she confided in her grandmother that she wanted to find her real mother, the woman who had parted with her at six weeks old. It was not that she didn't love her adoptive mum, she said. The new legal arrangements made it easier for Kelly to trace her mother, and at last a meeting was arranged. Kelly's mother wasn't a foreign princess or someone famous: she was a harassed mother with a brood of unruly boys. She was hoping that Kelly would turn out to be another pair of hands: there was nothing else on offer for her.

Kelly came home sobered and glad to have the parents and grandparents who had cared for her all her life. But the ghost was laid. This is a common outcome from such meetings, but it is important for the child's family not to feel hurt or offended by this assuaging of normal curiosity.

You, as a granny, and not so deeply involved, can help your son or daughter and partner keep such problems with ready-made children in perspective.

Ready-made Summary

- Blood and genes
- Adoption
- The other parent's children
- Part-time grandchildren
- Avoiding conflicts
- Four essential rules

Chapter 10
Special Children

Grandparents are doubly important when a grandchild is ill or has special problems. The ways in which you are so greatly needed are first and foremost psychological. The parents will need your sympathy, support, encouragement and practical good sense. You must be the unflappable one. You will notice that the most independent adult son or daughter, whose attitude towards you up till now has been one of kindly tolerance, suddenly seems to grow younger and looks to you for comfort and even advice.

Your grandchild, when he or she is sick, will also make emotional claims on you, and he too will have slipped back into a more dependent stage. This is a time for short-term babying, and longer term, for extra supplies of love and patience. If you live inconveniently far away, unless the situation is serious enough for you to up-sticks to visit the young family or stay nearby, you can still do a great deal that is useful by telephone and letter.

Hands-on help is pure gold in short-lived illnesses like an ear infection, or a crisis situation like appendicitis or an accident. It can be equally valuable in chronic disorders necessitating frequent trips to the hospital or centre, or practice exercises at home, from cerebral palsy to dyslexia.

EVERYDAY ILLNESSES

These are not serious, but bad enough for the child to be confined to bed or at least to one, warm room. The commonest are coughs and colds and 'flu, digestive upsets and a few specific infections, such as mumps, German measles and chicken-pox. The immunization

114

programme protects today's children from the other nasties, measles and whooping cough. Measles should soon be eradicated altogether if not too many opt out of the programme.

Ellie: looking back, had perhaps been quieter than usual for the last two or three days, but the spots came as a surprise. They were dark pink to start with, and in her scalp and on her chest, then under her arms. They turned to blisters in a matter of hours and were intensely itchy. New crops kept coming out every second day it seemed, mainly on her neck and body. Ellie was only four and she hadn't started school yet. No one in her playgroup had been ill, but the family had stayed with Uncle Joe and Aunty May the weekend before last. Aunty May had been complaining of a pain in her side while they were there, but she didn't begin to feel ill until the day after they had left. She had developed shingles.

Ellie wasn't really ill – she was too lively for that – but the chicken-pox had given her over 100 spots, all at different stages and all getting itchier and itchier until they finally turned into scabs. It was difficult to stop her scratching them and getting them infected, which would make the scars worse. Her mother rang up Ellie's granny, Madge, with an SOS. Could she possibly sit with Ellie for an hour while she did some vital shopping?

Madge set off with a jigsaw, a picture book and a bottle of apple juice. She also took some calamine lotion which the doctor had recommended and a small artist's paintbrush. Every single spot was painted individually, twice if it was naughty enough to itch after it had been done. It was a most satisfying ritual. Madge visited Ellie every day until the spots cleared up. Ellie loved her granny's company, Madge enjoyed spending time with her granddaughter and feeling needed, and Ellie's mum welcomed the chance to get on with everyday jobs.

With most ordinary illnesses, what you can do to help your grandchild is clear and straightforward. It is important not to forget the other sufferer. The anxious, often over-strained mum needs as big a dose of Tender Loving Care as the little patient.

Fathers, in the nature of things, are seldom left to carry the burden of nursing a sick child as well as coping with the usual washing, cooking and cleaning and either shopping or arranging for someone else to bring in supplies. There may be other children to fetch from school. If you can give the mother a break – even for coffee and Woman's Hour – you will be recharging her batteries. The bonus is that your grandchild will appreciate the time with you, partly because you do everything differently from his mother, and you will get to know each other more thoroughly than by 1000 'best behaviour' visits.

A working mother may run into special difficulties. Employers aren't monsters, but they are very often men without a clue about what having an ill child entails. If there is a risk that your daughter or daughter-in-law will feel she simply must go back to work, even if it means leaving the young invalid on his or her own for several hours, it is worth your making a major effort to plug the gap. It is definitely unsafe to leave a child of eleven or under without adult company, however sensible he or she is, and even if a neighbour says she will look in.

Mind you, it can still feel pretty miserable at fourteen to be left on your own for more than an hour or so, when you are ill.

Barry was twelve, a responsible young fellow, and he assured his mother that he would be quite OK on his own while she was at work. She left him his lunch on a tray, and plenty of biscuits and fruit for snacks, a bottle of lemon barley and a thermos of hot chocolate – his favourite. He had books and the radio by his bed.

Barry was getting over glandular fever. Although in the early stages his mum had taken time off from her job as a sales representative, her boss was getting edgy and she herself felt she was losing touch with the clients. She didn't like it, but she felt it was safe to leave Barry now. Besides, she didn't want to bother Carrie, her mother-in-law: she wasn't young and it meant a tiresome bus ride for her to get to their house.

Carrie was startled to hear Barry's tearful voice on the phone. He'd had what seemed a good idea – bringing the TV set upstairs from the drawing room. On the way up he suddenly felt dizzy (not unusual even weeks after an attack of glandular fever), a trailing wire got tangled in his foot, the TV set began to slip and Barry lost his balance. The TV was smashed in the fall and he had hit his head and it had gone a funny shape. He couldn't ring Mum because she'd be out seeing clients. Carrie was speeding across town in a cab in no time, her arthritis for once forgotten.

Barry was a sorry sight, with a big lump on his forehead, but nothing else that hurt or felt funny. Carrie had seen bumps like this when her own boys were young and always in the wars. She sent Barry back to bed, found a pack of frozen peas in the fridge and wrapped it in a tea towel to put on the swelling. Then she telephoned the doctor, who asked a few questions and said that Carrie had done exactly the right thing and she herself would call in later. By the time she came the lump was much smaller, but she said Barry might develop a black eye. He was rather pleased about that.

It is an insurance to teach your grandchildren your telephone number, and to give them some practice – for fun – in ringing you up.

LONG-TERM PROBLEMS

These can affect the whole family and the child's future – and they call for your top-quality grannying skills. When a child is born with some imperfection the effect on the parents is devastating. They are riven with sadness, humiliation – and guilt. Grandparents expecting a beautiful, perfect grandchild to coo over and boast about are upset, too. They may even feel ashamed. But a granny must not let her feelings of disappointment show. Her role as wise counsellor and provider of instant support is vital from the day it is realized that there is a problem. She has also got to ensure that the grandfather in the case – her husband – is equally sensitive in his reaction.

Maggie and Ted were a carefree young couple, still on a high of love after two years of marriage. They were thrilled when the ultrasound showed that they would soon have a dear little daughter. Dora, one of the grannies-to-be, went on a shopping splurge of tiny frilly dresses to make up for the boring, unisex Babygro suits that Maggie had bought. The baby was to be called Angelica.

The labour was not overlong and Ted was at hand with strict instructions to let Dora know as soon as she was a granny: she would be waiting by the telephone. The midwife was oddly quiet at what should have been her moment of triumph. 'A healthy little girl,' she said at last. Baby Angie had a cleft lip, and her face looked, frankly, horrifying. Although Ted had forewarned her, Dora's first sight of Angie was a shock. She felt that she wanted to blame something, someone – had her daughter-in-law done something wrong during the pregnancy? However, when she saw poor Maggie's stricken expression, with the tear-tracks still showing, she hugged her tightly, and said what a sweetheart little Angie was and that she couldn't have loved her more.

Dora, truth to tell, hadn't been over-keen to be a grandmother. She was only forty-five and had the figure of a twenty-year-old. Appearances had always mattered to her and the embarrassment of having this caricature of a granddaughter almost outweighed her feeling of pity and protectiveness towards the baby and all she and her parents would have to go through. The first, vital operation to give Angie anything like a normal mouth could not be undertaken until she was three months old. Meanwhile, she was a nightmare to try to feed, and friends and other people turned away sharply when they peeped into the crib or pram.

Of course it came right in the end. Angie had to have several operations during her childhood, but she grew into a pretty girl with only the thinnest line across her lip to remind those who had known her of the sufferings of the past. By then Dora had got used to being a granny – and important to the family. She also had the satisfaction of knowing that she had played her part really well, even when it had meant a huge effort. She had been the model of a loving grandmother, holding the little *scrap in her arms, mopping up the endless dribbles neatly and unobtrusively, and murmuring that she was the best, dearest baby in the world. Ted and Maggie never knew how much Dora had to pretend at first, but her warm, accepting attitude helped their own hurt more than all the doctors' reassurance. Dora is a very well-loved granny.*

Although a baby may be born with a problem as serious as cerebral palsy or mental handicap, unlike Angie's condition, it may not be obvious straightaway. This can mean weeks or months when the parents feel that something is wrong but cannot pinpoint it, when they hold their breath and hope. Sometimes you as a granny sense the underlying anxiety and can help the mother or father – depending on which is closest to you – to tell you their fears and doubts. Your support is a wonderful comfort during this phase of uncertainty, but it is sensible not to overdo the reassurance. If you insist that everything about the baby is normal and perfect – just slow development – and then he turns out to be spastic, your opinion will have lost its value for the future.

Moira's second grandchild was the boy his parents had wanted: a good-looking young fellow they called Ben. Cleo had gone through a somewhat protracted labour to produce him, because the cord had got looped round his neck, holding up his progress. However, he seemed none the worse. He was a good baby: he seldom cried and didn't move around much, so his bedclothes stayed tidy all night. One snag: he was an agonizingly slow feeder – not a bit like his big sister, Emmie, aged two. She had been a lively, hungry infant and had kept her parents awake many nights.

Cleo felt uneasy but she didn't tell Moira. This was partly so as not to worry her, partly because she was afraid to put her fear into words and partly because if there was anything wrong with her baby she would feel ashamed. Jeff just thought they were lucky – or clever – to have such an easy child.

Over the next weeks Ben's floppy limbs and wobbly neck

became unmistakably abnormal. Cleo didn't tell Jeff how worried she was, and she didn't ask her mother to go with her when she took Ben to the specialist. Moira had no idea what was happening, and felt rather hurt that Cleo did not seem to want to share anything to do with the baby with her. When the diagnosis emerged for definite, that Ben had cerebral palsy, it meant frequent trips to the hospital and more to the physiotherapy clinic. His floppy muscles were now tightening up into a spastic condition.

Moira was very sympathetic when she was told that Ben was mildly spastic and would need special treatment, but Cleo brushed the problems aside. Her mother did not realize the slogging effort involved in getting Ben to his appointments by public transport, with a lively toddler tagging along too. She did not realize, either, that finding that you haven't got the perfect child you'd planned for is like a bereavement. She did not guess the waves of guilt and resentment that engulfed Cleo, and her difficulty in accepting Ben as he actually was.

This is an 'if only' story. If only Moira had known the situation early on, she could have helped her daughter through the phase of fear and doubts, and supported her in her despair when she knew the diagnosis by listening and discussing and comforting. She could have lent a practical hand by going with Cleo on the trains and buses with the baby, the buggy and the toddler. She could have 'borrowed' her granddaughter for a few hours so that Cleo could get about with Ben more easily, and she could have learned to help with Ben's exercises.

Moira missed out on a good deal that she could have done for Ben and his parents when he was little, because of Cleo's pride and poor communication between family members who all cared for one another. At least she was there and ready with support at the second crunch period. Like many youngsters with physical problems, Ben went through a rough patch when he was an adolescent. He had no confidence when it came to the boyfriend/girlfriend stakes – and needed every possible boost to his self-esteem.

If your grandchild has the bad luck to be only 90 per cent perfect he will need your love and patience, and particularly your encouragement, to be as independent as possible. The paediatricians say that overprotective mothers and grannies are the fourth handicap. Children usually take any disabilities phlegmatically and enjoy to the full all that they can do. It is the mothers who need the sympathy, the cossetting and the little presents.

Molly was mildly mentally handicapped. She did not have Down's syndrome or the small-sized head that would have been instantly recognizable to the doctors, so no one considered the possibility of such a problem to start with. Her parents had waited for some years before they felt ready to start a family: it was no casual decision. The test for Down's was negative and the pregnancy and labour went according to plan. The usual tests for thyroid deficiency and phenylketonuria shortly after she was born were also negative.

Molly was a contented baby. Her father said that she knew when she was well off – with every need provided. The trouble was that she remained contented, when most babies are busy discovering their hands and toes, and craning their necks to get a glimpse of the world around. She was a little behind with her milestones, although that need not mean anything – but she didn't seem interested. Her family, parents and grandparents alike, wondered whether they should worry. Hearing and sight tests showed Molly to be normal in these respects. So they weren't the reason for Molly's delay in learning to talk. At two she was still making babyish babbling noises.

Mental handicap, which by definition calls for special educational help, can affect any family. In the vast majority of cases no cause can be identified. Molly's parents asked the age-old question, 'Why should this have happened to us?' There was no answer, no one and nothing to blame – and no miracle cure.

Molly's granny, June, was a pillar of strength in a situation which had undermined the parents' faith in themselves and in the future. It would have been tempting for June to have offered

*the wrong kind of comfort: encouraging a pretence that there
was nothing wrong with Molly, that she was just a slow
developer and much more 'knowing' than she appeared.
Some friends, out of kindness, used this line; others were
patronizing, and some mothers treated Molly and her parents
as though she had some contagious disease.*

*One of the embarrassing aspects arose when Molly was
about five. In her loud clear voice – at church, in the
supermarket, in the street or visiting friends – she would
say exactly what she thought about people, including strangers,
food she had been given, and places, such as friends' houses. At
five this wasn't so bad, but it continued as she became older –
eight and ten. It helped to have June's loyal support and that
she was often around to take Molly off 'for a little walk' or on
some other pretext. She never criticized: the family's feelings
were too tender for that.*

Long-term Planning

With any handicapped child the future must be mapped in
advance, not left to chance or the whim of the moment. There
are various things that you need to find out about schools and
facilities, costs and the policy of the local authority and other
centres. What sort of school will be needed for this particular
child? Would a boarding school provide the best training? What
special holidays are available.

As a granny you can act as a sounding board but whatever your
views, remember that this is not your own child, and powerful
emotions are in play. Don't press your own view. If boarding
school and separate holidays geared to children with your
grandchild's particular problems are chosen, do your utmost
not to let your daughter or daughter-in-law feel guilty that she
is not planning to be with her child twenty-four hours a day, seven
days a week – all year round. Handicapped children grow up into
adults, inescapably, and need to practise independence from
home and the ability to get on with other people.

Mentally handicapped children are not usually lacking emotionally and are often hurt more easily than people realize. If they

are made to feel clumsy, slow and stupid, and other people take over impatiently when, for instance, a child is putting on a shoe, the result is an unhappy youngster who won't even try. This situation calls for expert grannying. With your extra maturity it is for you to give the lead: by consistent good humour and patience. It is worthwhile remembering that playing a five-year-old's game, with a five-year-old if possible, can be normal for a twelve-year-old who is handicapped. Other people may find it odd, so you need to explain.

It is easier for the granny or mother of a child with Down's syndrome, because the characteristic appearance does the explaining for them.

GIFTED CHILDREN

Penny's problem was the opposite of Molly's. We all think our grandchildren are particularly intelligent, but Penny was super-bright. That was fine for her first two years. It meant that she passed the milestones of talking, walking and toilet control in record time. At three it seemed that she never stopped asking questions, and she insisted on learning her letters so that she could read. Of course her parents were thrilled, even if an afternoon with their daughter was exhausting.

Now the problems began. Penny was a trouble-maker at her nursery school. She was bored with colouring, threading beads on a bootlace, or growing a broad bean in a glass jar. She wanted to know – really – about dinosaurs, and Africa, kings and the ozone layer. From being sunny and interested in everything, she changed into an awkward, defiant little girl. At school she scribbled all over the wall and at home she wouldn't eat her dinner and she fought over going to bed. Granny Matthews, who had been a teacher, took turns in giving Penny's parents a break, by taking her on the sort of expeditions considered suitable for schoolchildren: to various museums, exhibitions and galleries.

Greg, Penny's father, approached Mensa and found that there was a special organization for the parents of gifted children. They were able to provide some useful information, but it became increasingly clear that the state education system would come nowhere near to satisfying Penny's needs. Special lessons were only available to those whose standard came below the norm. Yet if Penny continued being frustrated she would be likely to develop serious behavioural problems.

When she was older there might be scholarships she could take, but in the early years the only way that she could obtain the type of education she needed was by paying hefty fees. For Granny Matthews, a widow with a fixed income, it was difficult for her to contribute, but the other grandparents and Greg managed to scrape enough together. It didn't seem fair that a dull child may receive state help, but there is nothing for the child who is too clever.

SOME LESSER PROBLEMS

Eczema
This condition can make a baby restless, irritable and miserable.

Yvonne was mortified that however gentle she was, her young grandson, Selwyn, screamed if she gave him a little cuddle. His skin was so sore. Yet it seemed cruel and unnatural not to hold or touch the baby; besides, even when he was left alone at night, for example, he was restless and often cried from the irritation of his eczema. Of course the doctor had given his parents some ointment to apply, and he told them that they must make every effort to stop Selwyn scratching.

In practice that meant that by the time he could sit up he could never be left to play by himself for a little while. Instead he had to be carried round and amused and distracted non-stop by whoever was looking after him, usually his mother. She was exhausted. Selwyn's face looked a mess with sore, red cheeks, and everything was smeared with ointment. Yvonne lent a hand whenever she could, which involved making a patchwork of her life. She tried to do it calmly, because eczema, like other allergies, is made worse by any emotional *tension. As well as being a toddler's entertainer, Yvonne had to become expert at smoothing ruffled feelings – usually her poor daughter's, Selwyn's mother. The one consoling thought was that infantile eczema usually clears up by the time the child is two or three.*

Asthma

Like eczema and hay fever, asthma is an allergy that runs in families. As well as the inborn tendency, there is frequently a reaction to the house dust mite and always an emotional element. Asthma has been on the increase since the Second World War, partly due to the stress of modern life, as it affects children, and partly due to pollution.

Pam's granddaughter, Debbie, developed asthma when she was ten. It came out of the blue. She was an especially precious child because she'd had pneumonia as a baby and nearly died. Pam couldn't blame her daughter for being extra fussy now, nor, for that matter, her son-in-law who had been asthmatic himself. As someone who felt he knew, he tried to lay down clear rules for Debbie to avoid bringing on an asthma attack. They included not playing with anyone who had a snuffle, not going out in a cold east wind, not taking part in school games, and watching her diet.

All these were sensible, but Pam could see that, now she was getting older, Debbie felt suffocated by her parents' concern. Of course, over-energetic exercise or catching an infection could set off an attack, but Pam couldn't help noticing that Debbie's asthma seemed to be much worse at weekends, when she was with her parents, than during the school week. Pam could not criticize Debbie's poor, worried parents but she did point out that there was no reason why the child should not go swimming with the school. It is the one form of exercise recommended by the experts as unlikely to cause an attack.

Pam also reminded them all that asthma is not really an illness, but a temporary reaction to some irritant – and a thorough nuisance. What would have been the worst possible

situation for Debbie would have been for her granny, as well as
her parents, to show their anxiety whenever Debbie coughed or
wheezed and in between times to remind her to be careful.
There is a natural tendency for childhood asthma to get better
in adolescence, so it is sensible for parents and grandparents to
take a more relaxed attitude as the youngster grows older.

Dyslexia

This condition is one reason for a child's doing badly at school.
Especially if he or she seems bright, his or her difficulty with
reading and writing may be put down to laziness. Most dyslexics
have had an unhappy time at school. This makes it all the more
important that dyslexia should be recognized. Extra, individual
lessons to help him – or, less often, her – over his particular
difficulty are effective. The condition can be cured.

Grannies and parents can help by practising with any child who
is having problems over reading. A big dose of love and praise and
sympathy should be part of each session, because the child's
teachers are certain to have shown their exasperation with him. It
doesn't matter whether or not your grandchild has true dyslexia or
is just a bad speller – the same method helps. It is sometimes
helpful to explain that writing is only talking on paper, not a secret
code for clever people.

Poor Hearing and Short Sight

These are other common reasons to consider when a child who
seems bright enough is making a lot of mistakes in his school
work, put down to carelessness. It is natural for you as a granny to
find excuses for your grandchild, even when he is genuinely
naughty – but sometimes you may be the one to uncover a
physical problem that hadn't been spotted. It may not have caused
any noticeable trouble in the early, easy stages of school.

KEY POINTS FOR GRANNIES WITH SPECIAL GRANDCHILDREN

- patience with the child
- unfailing affection and a sense of humour

- understanding and sympathy for the parents, who will feel guilty, ashamed and sad if their child is less than perfect
- instant availability of support when needed (practical or psychological), but the gift of fading into the background when you are not needed

Special Children Summary

- When a grandchild is sick
- Everyday illnesses
- Cleft lip
- Cerebral palsy
- Mental handicap
- Eczema
- Asthma
- Dyslexia

Chapter 11

What Happens When We Die?

WE HAVE a natural instinct to shield the children we love from anything frightening, upsetting, sad or unpleasant. That seems to rule out death. In fact, in our Western culture that is what we try to do, even among adults. There is a conspiracy of silence about dying, as there was about sex for the Victorians. Mourning is done in private: no longer the black clothes or at least an armband, or the withdrawal from social life that let other people know we are bereaved. If we do have to talk about the D word, we use euphemisms: the 'dear departed' has 'passed away', 'gone to his eternal rest' or 'gone to sleep'.

We would prefer to pretend to little children that there is no such thing as death, but you can't prevent them from seeing a dead fledgling that has fallen from its nest or a hedgehog squashed in the road. And they will have overheard grown-ups talking in a special voice about people who have died. There isn't a hope of fobbing off a normal child's curiosity about death. From the time that they can hold a conversation they are interested in the subject, and will ask those penetrating, straight-to-the-point questions:

'When will you die, Granny?'
'Does it hurt?'
'What happens after you're dead?'

As a granny, someone so old that you are expected to know everything about this subject, you are likely to be targeted. You need to have your answers ready: honest and informative, with no prevarication. It is cheating to say: 'Ask me another time – I'm busy' or 'Wait until you are older – you'll be able to understand it then.'

Death is something we all have to come to terms with sooner or later, and children need our help and guidance with how to deal with it. There are two aspects of death that children find particularly difficult: its permanence and its inevitability. When children say 'Bang, bang! You're dead' they expect their playmate to get up and continue the game. Death and disaster on TV convey a similar idea. A child soon learns that when the hero is shot, he is never killed, and the actor playing the thug who gets his come-uppance in the final scene will be up to his thuggery again in another film.

This problem with appreciating the reality of death has led to some appalling tragedies in the United States, where ordinary families may keep guns in their homes. Tinies of three and five have shot their mothers and other children dead and shown surprise that they didn't get up again – ever. It is never too soon to put across the permanence of death.

It is because children can find it difficult to believe in the seriousness of death that they often appear callous when someone close to them dies. This is especially noticeable among the five to eight-year-olds. They can talk about the event logically enough, but are not able to grasp its emotional significance.

In a trivial way it can jar on our adult sensibilities when a child seems more interested than sorry at the sight of a dead animal. My grandson brought a dead blackbird in from the garden to show us. There was no hint of the squeamishness I would have felt in handling it – he wanted us to see its feet and wings. Of course, some children will react in the way we adults expect, with tears and pity – my granddaughter at two even tried to kiss a dead sparrow better. Don't misjudge your grandchild as heartless if his or her reaction is the scientific one: it's a matter of emotional maturity.

It is natural that all of us, youngsters or oldies, should be afraid of losing someone we are fond of. This thought can haunt a child who is beginning to understand that old people die, and occasionally younger ones. A grandchild may look at you anxiously, wondering if you will last till Christmas, when you have some minor illness. To children, grandparents are very old indeed – even if they are barely fifty. It is a frightening realization at any age that we ourselves are mortal. This doesn't usually strike children until they are in their teens, unless they have heard about the death of some other child. The much-publicized medical cases that don't have a happy ending can set off the fear.

How to explain death

Death is an even dodgier subject than sex to explain to children; and it is more likely that we grannies will be called upon for the information since we are the nearest to the event. You don't want to make it frightening, but there are some pitfalls to sidestep. For example, you may make a timid child more nervous if you liken death to a lovely, long, peaceful sleep.

Louise, at seven, sat up all night when she heard this. She was terrified that if she fell asleep she might never wake up, but Bobby, her brother, wondered if you had to clean your teeth and put on your pyjamas before you died.

Along similar lines, never pretend to a child who is upset at the sight of a dead animal, whether wild or a pet, that the creature is asleep. If this is sleep, they don't want to experience it. It is better to explain briefly that the animal must have been too badly injured or ill to be able to live, but that nothing is hurting it now, or ever will.

You might think it easier and more reassuring if you bring religion into the death question. Unless the whole family is devout and certain in its beliefs, it can be a minefield. Vague descriptions of an afterlife with God can sound mysterious and alarming. You may personalize it and say that dear Jesus comes specially to gather up the sick person in his arms and carry them to his house to make them well and happy forever. This may be reminiscent of something a child has heard at school or on the news, about social workers swooping down to take children into care, away from their mothers and fathers. There is never anything on TV about people going to Jesus' place.

Even if personally you are confident that there is a happy life for everyone after death, your grandchild will hear other views at school, and yet more as a teenager, when youngsters are working out their own philosophy. If he or she develops doubts, he cannot discuss them with you if your beliefs are set in stone.

Most of us do not have this cast-iron certainty of an afterlife, but it is worse than useless to tell a child something important if you do not believe it. She won't be able to pinpoint what is wrong with what you say, but she will pick up your unease. It is safer to admit that you don't know for certain what happens after somebody dies, but you can truthfully say that death itself isn't painful – even if the person had an unpleasant illness beforehand. The other consolation is memory. Death is not the end of someone you love, because you can remember such a lot about them – and even know what they would have said if they had been present.

At all ages it is helpful to talk openly to children about death. Any concept that has become familiar loses its power to frighten. Children take it for granted that when they are five they will go to proper school, and when they are grown-up they won't live at home. This is because they have had a long time to get used to the idea, and it happens to everyone: just like death. A common error is to tell children that only old people die: they are sure to find out that you are wrong and your credibility is out of the window. Of course you can say that it is exceptional for a young person to die. The main object is to teach your grandchildren to love life and enjoy it to the full, but not to fear death.

WHEN A PET DIES

This is usually a child's first personal bereavement. Hamsters have a high mortality rate and although it is sad when they die, it hasn't the impact of the loss of a dog or cat who has been part of the family.

Nicky had a black and white kitten called Pinky. Nicky was five and she and Pinky had frolicking games all over the house with balls of paper and pieces of string. They were playmates. Then Pinky slipped out of the front door one day and ran into the path of a passing car. Nicky was heartbroken. Her mother would have disposed of the body herself, discreetly, and was already promising a replacement – thinking to help Nicky get over the tragedy almost before she had realized it.

Her granny was wiser. She persuaded Nicky's mother that some tears and sadness were natural and healthy, and would help to wash the hurt away. All three of them chose a pretty, peaceful corner of the garden and buried Pinky there, snugly wrapped in a piece of blanket. Nicky said 'Bye-bye, Pinky' and put some flower petals on the earth in the shape of a P. There were still a few tears but Nicky felt a solemn satisfaction at having done all she could for Pinky, even in death.

Then she asked Granny the unanswerable question – for most of us: 'What will happen to Pinky now?' It would have been easy to say that Pinky would be going to a cat heaven with saucers of milk galore and pieces of string to chase – and that they would meet again one day in the long-distant future. Instead, Nicky's granny said that she did not really know, but it was good that Pinky had such a lot of fun, and Nicky could always remember that she had helped to give the little kitten a very happy life.

If Nicky's mother had followed her immediate impulse after Pinky's accident, she would have tried to pretend that Pinky had gone away, and she would have bought another kitten straightaway. That would have left Nicky confused and with her sad feelings bottled up inside. If a child is old enough to talk it is always a therapy to put feelings of upset into words and share them with someone warm and loving.

The death of a pet can provide valuable lessons and practice in coping with bereavement. Handled the right way it will stand the child in good stead when there are more serious losses later in his or her life.

DEATH OF A GRANDPARENT, AUNT OR UNCLE

It is not unusual for even a young child to go through the experience of losing someone dear to them by death, and the likeliest person is a grandparent. The grandmother or grandfather may have been ill or failing for some time, and it is important that the child should not be kept in the dark. Just as for an adult, it makes it easier to come to terms with a person's death if there has been some forewarning. It may be that a grandfather or the other grandmother dies, and among other trains of thought, your grandchild may wonder if you will be next.

Zach had enjoyed fun times with his grandfather who was only sixty-three when he had his second, fatal, heart attack. Most of us, when we are bereaved, feel guilty that we didn't do enough for the dead person or that some years-old misunderstanding hadn't been resolved. It is emotional, not logical. Young children can also feel guilty. Zach was four, young enough to believe that he might have caused his grandfather's death by not being a good boy. Added to that, he had not even said 'Goodbye' before his grandpa died. To counteract the possible effects of his badness on other members of the family, Zach became extra good. It was unnatural, but Gran, whose husband it was that had died, guessed the reason.

She broached the subject which everyone else had avoided mentioning when Zach was there:

'We miss Granpy, don't we?'

'We wish he was still alive.'

Once the ice was broken, Gran was able to help Zach talk about how he felt, and she told him how we always tend to feel that it must somehow be our fault when someone special dies: but that we are not truly to blame. It is just part of feeling sad. Gran said it didn't matter not saying 'Goodbye', but Zach sorted that out for himself. After a lot of discussion it was decided to take Zach along to the funeral. It was a brief affair in the crematorium chapel. When all the good things about the dead man had been said, the coffin began to move between the curtains. Zach's high voice rang out:

'Goodbye, Granpy.'

Even if it had not provided such a healing opportunity, it was a wise choice to let the little boy share the adults' grief and their more formal farewell. Zach did not need to stay super-good after the ceremony. He asked if Granpy still loved him and was reassured to learn that love is something that goes on for always. After all, he hadn't stopped loving Granpy just because he'd died. It helps a young child – and you – if you don't hide your grief but share it. It makes matters worse if we try to prevent little ones from expressing their feelings – of sorrow, puzzlement or anger at the unfairness of death.

Older children often have a close, supportive relationship with a grandparent, and their death means the loss of a confidant and counsellor. These youngsters in particular need interest and encouragement from the other adults in the family. They also need to know that any feelings of guilt are not unusual, but certainly unjustified.

Your Death

In the open talk about death which all the child psychologists recommend, your grandchild may ask you when you are going to die, where you will go then, and if you are afraid. Don't duck these questions: they are serious and indicate concern for you. It is always best to be truthful, however brief your answers. Children are realists. Unless you are actually mortally ill, in which case you can say that you are getting rather tired, your best line is to talk about what you enjoy in your life, but that you have had quite a long turn already. There are new people being born, and in the end your turn will be up: of course you will be sorry, but it is fair, and nothing to be afraid of.

The key word is openness. It can be disastrous, however kind your motives, to hide the facts of death from a child.

DEATH OF A PARENT

Evie was eleven, just about to change schools. The family had just enjoyed a holiday in the Lakes, and they had come back tanned and, they thought, fit. True, Alastair, her father, had his blood pressure to contend with, but he was on medication and he was only fifty-two. It was Evie who found him, slumped on the floor by the loft ladder: he had been taking some boxes up. Of course, her mother and the 'aunty' from next door got him to bed and called the doctor. Her big brother came home from college, but to Evie's enormous puzzlement she was sent off to stay with her granny, her mother's mother, for a week. Granny had been over-persuaded into a foolish conspiracy. Alastair was dead, but they told Evie that he was ill and had gone to hospital.

When the adults' first reaction of grief and shock had subsided and the funeral was safely over, they told Evie that her daddy had died in the hospital, in his sleep. He was now in Heaven and perfectly happy. The story was obviously phoney but no one would answer Evie's questions. Worse still, all the adults hid their sadness and shushed Evie when she tried to express hers: Daddy was in a happy place and would not want her to cry.

Evie's unresolved grief could have pushed her into a physical illness or a depression. In the event, she reacted by acting up. She was stroppy and sullen by turns and at her new school she acquired the reputation of being wild, and always at the centre of some trouble. It was when she came home with some cannabis that the family realized that they may have handled Evie's father's death wrongly. A child psychiatrist helped them all, including the grandmother, at last to discuss openly their feelings about Alastair's death, both the negative and the conventional kind.

The death of a parent involves special problems. The widowed parent is stricken with personal grief, just when the child needs most reassurance. Evie's mother, intending to save the child distress while she dealt with the funeral and other necessary arrangements, seemed to be abandoning her by sending her to Granny's. When Evie came back her mother went through the normal physical caring for her, but hid her own emotional upset. This only served to confuse and frighten Evie. It is essential for a child to be allowed to mourn, to work through the stages of grief like the rest of us. If this does not happen there is a definite risk of the child's developing a serious depression as an adolescent or even later. With her mother withdrawing emotionally it was as if Evie had lost both parents.

The long-term problems for a family in which the father has died are likely to include money. Evie's mother had to change her part-time job for full-time, so in this crucial period she had less time available for her daughter. Her own mother was needed more than ever to fill in some of the gaps, so that Evie had a grown-up to rely on.

The death of a mother is often more disrupting to a child's life than losing his father.

Bryn's father had a good job but he could not have afforded a nanny and housekeeper to look after the two-year-old after his mother was killed in a road accident. At first Bryn was shuttled from one relative to another – they were all busy people, with other commitments. What he desperately needed was one steady person, not a great expert, but someone interested in him and his progress. It was important not to delay the long-term arrangements.

After a great deal of discussion, Bryn's granny, his father's mother, agreed to give up her office job and look after Bryn from Monday to Friday, office hours, for whatever his father could afford. His dad would have to cope with the weekends. It worked out quite well, and it was easier for Bryn to attach his love and dependence to the granny he already knew than to a stranger. In due course Bryn's dad built a relationship with a woman he met at a Gingerbread group – an outfit for lone parents. She had a little daughter. They all got to know each other, including Granny, and a marriage is in the offing.

DEATH OF A BROTHER OR SISTER

If this tragedy strikes a family it is likely that the child who dies is very young. It is particularly common for the child who is alive to feel guilty – a form of survivor guilt. Often the dead child is never mentioned, which only makes matters worse. A granny can help her grandchild by encouraging him to talk and ask about anything that worries him, including any subject which seems taboo at home.

SICK CHILDREN

Children, especially those over ten, are frequently afraid that they are going to die, if for any reason they have to go to hospital. Often they don't say anything to their parents, because they don't want to upset them.

> Liz was nine when she had one of her severe asthma attacks and was admitted to hospital. Asthma itself is frightening, and added to that Liz knew from experience that people died in hospitals. Both her grandfathers had done so. It was Liz's chatty granny who enabled the subject of Liz's anxiety to come into the open. She was able to tell the nurses of her granddaughter's need for authoritative reassurance.

When a child is gravely ill and likely to die, if there is even the remotest chance of recovery, it is worth focusing on that. In the completely no-hope situation, if the child hasn't realized and doesn't seem worried, it is usually better to remain generally encouraging. Just occasionally, however, a child knows that he is dying and needs to talk about it. It is a relief to him to be allowed to express his feelings and to ask about anything he is unsure of.

> Dominic was twelve, and he was dying of leukaemia. All the treatment options had been used up and he was getting weaker. He asked his doctor when he was going to die. It wasn't that Dominic couldn't accept the fact, but he was in the middle of doing a big painting and he wanted to be able to finish it. He did.
>
> His grandmother's job was to comfort his heartbroken parents and reassure them, again and again, that they had done absolutely everything they could.

What Happens When We Die? Summary

- Don't try to fob them off
- Meeting the reality of death
- Explaining death
- Death of a family pet
- Talking about the dead person
- Sick children and hospital

Chapter 12
Your Turn

For ELEVEN CHAPTERS we have been concentrating on what you can do for your grandchild, what is best for the other people in your family. It's a reflection of your life: like most women with children and grandchildren, you will have put yourself last all these years. It mustn't be a habit. Now is the time when you should study your needs, your wishes, for once – and that is what this chapter is about.

You will already have noticed that getting older is not what you'd thought. The day you are fifty or sixty or seventy – or these days even eighty – you don't suddenly feel different. Nor do other people start treating you with extra consideration, let alone veneration. Nevertheless, any of these decade milestones is a reminder to take stock. There are two major life events that will have an impact:

1. If you are a working woman, there may be a compulsory age for retirement, or you may be 'offered' early retirement any time from fifty, in such a way that you have no choice.
2. You become a grandmother.

These two events can interact. If you no longer have an outside job you may feel that having a lot more spare time will fit in marvellously with all the pleasures and duties of being a granny. Or you may feel in danger of being trapped: with no excuse not to look after the howling, leaky bundle whenever its parents want a break. Perhaps you look forward hopefully to one of the following scenarios?

1. Spending oodles of time with your children and grand-children: a welcome and well-loved part of their lives. For yourself you will enjoy over again the fun and fascination of helping a little child grow and learn.

2. Having no ties, you move home to be near your children and grandchildren. You are independent and can get away when you are tired, yet you can pop in whenever you feel like it.

3. Particularly if you are widowed, you think it sensible to pool your resources to allow for fixing up a granny flat in your son's or daughter's house. You are on the spot, but you have your own front door – it could be handy if you, or one of them, are ill.

4. This one applies particularly if you have a partner to feed: regular visits to your place by the whole family – say every Sunday for a proper lunch. And of course, you will expect them to come to you for Christmas, Easter and any special birthday. Perhaps you'll all go on holiday together.

5. Breaking the monotony of being on your own by staying with your daughter or daughter-in-law and the family for a week or two now and again – say three or four times a year. Of course, they'll look forward to your visit as much as you do, and be loath to part with you when you finally tear yourself away.

6. You've worked hard all your life, made sacrifices and done everything for your family all the years that they couldn't fend for themselves. Now they'll want to look after you – at least provide transport, do a bit of DIY and be available when any problem crops up: like the fridge won't work or you can't understand your income tax form.

If any of these possibilities is in your mind, or actually on offer from the younger generation, have a long, hard think. Each of these situations has been played out in a TV sit-com, but they are not so funny in real life. Your children and your grandchildren love you enormously and value you greatly. They want you to be happy, and if you aren't they will feel guilty: especially if you let slip that you are sometimes lonely. Loneliness acts like blackmail: it induces people to give up things they value, in this case their privacy and independence.

Modern life and modern attitudes simply don't chime in with the cosy Victorian idea of a closely interwoven extended family. It doesn't even work in Italy today, where traditionally a family without a live-in grandmother was incomplete. The generation gap itself is irrelevant: too much of anybody else would be just as much of a strain on the family. Nowadays, marriages and partnerships are so fragile that the additional stress of a mother-in-law on the scene – or on the phone – may be the fatal straw. You cannot avoid being the mother-in-law of one of your grandchild's parents. Even a grandchild who loves you may find it surprisingly wearing and frustrating if, for example, every Sunday is given over to you.

Joanna was close to her mother, and her mother was close to Granny, who was now sixty-eight. Granny had been a wonderful help minding Joanna in her pre-school years so that her mother could go out to work. Now she spent a lot of her time with Joanna's family, especially at weekends. You couldn't plan anything without including her. Joanna was fifteen and working for her GCSEs. She felt as though she had two fussy mothers telling her what to do – although she was nearly grown-up. Granny's going on at her about her eating – 'you're a growing girl' – was irritating beyond endurance.

Joanna developed bulimia nervosa, and did not begin to get better until the family instituted a new regime and Granny only visited when she was invited to something special. In fact she became a leading light in the Townswomen's Guild and the local U3A, and was often too busy.

Dolly and Lilian reached their disagreeable situation in a more typical way. Dolly had a miserable first marriage, short-lived and with no children. She was delighted when, at thirty-nine, she met Mark, a bachelor of forty-two, who was definitely interested. He had never married, partly because he was too comfortable living with his widowed mother, Lilian, and partly because he didn't like to leave her. Lilian herself had always said that she wanted Mark to marry, and indeed she did all she could to encourage the relationship with Dolly.

Lilian was over the moon when Dolly became pregnant and thrilled with little Sonya, the grandchild she had thought she would never have. Lilian was a kind, generous granny to the little girl. When Sonya was ten, Lilian was seventy-six and having increasing trouble with her arthritis. Dolly was only too glad to fit in her mother-in-law's shopping, often in the lunch break, when the latter was having difficulty in getting to the shops. She found herself drawn in to doing more and more of Lilian's housework, taking her to the doctor's, and then regularly to physio.

Dolly didn't grudge the effort – at first – but she began to feel as though she were on a treadmill. Although Mark was the major breadwinner, Dolly too had a job, and of course the flat and Sonya to look after. When she explained to Mark he suggested that it might make it easier all round if his mother moved in with them. Dolly could have screamed, but she did not want to upset Mark nor hurt Lilian's feelings, so she tried reasoning. Mark, of course, could see no problem: he'd lived with his mother for forty-two years. Similarly, Lilian had no qualms about the arrangement.

The tension in the flat rose as soon as Lilian moved in; Dolly found that she was even being irritable with Sonya, she couldn't talk to Mark and she felt like an outsider. Then Lilian had a fall and broke her hip. Dolly was adamant that she could not come back to the flat. Lilian was found a place in sheltered accommodation: a group of bungalows with a warden, a nurse and meals provided if necessary. If Lilian had suggested this solution to her health problems herself her son would not have felt guilty towards her and resentful towards his wife; Sonya would have lived in a happier home.

You may be a grandmother before your time: that is, you are up to your eyes in business or other affairs and none of the six nightmare possibilities applies. There's no way you want closer integration – you simply don't have the time. You may even feel somewhat lacking on the grandmother front – you haven't done much dandling of an adoring grandchild on your knee, nor turned up religiously at every school play or sports day. Celebrate the situation!

As well as living your own useful existence, you are providing a brilliant model of maturity for your grandchildren to emulate, growing up in the twenty-first century. My children much preferred the granny who ran a shop and wouldn't allow any playing about there, to the lady-of-leisure granny who liked to take them on shopping trips.

If you are not a fifty- or sixty-year-old business whizz kid, could you fit any of the stereotypes of grandmothers, or women of grandmother age, on TV or in books? For example, there is the intimidating mother-in-law variety, who also intimidates her grand-children; the foolish, feather-brained ditherer, who wouldn't even know what a CD-ROM is; a sentimental, spoiling granny who believes that children are all little angels and undermines everything that responsible parents try to do; and the final insult – the comical cleaning lady. Of course not: none of these is remotely like you.

Take it that you are an average, ordinary woman who has grandchildren but is no longer subject to the constant demands of bringing up her own growing children, or fitting a career round a million other responsibilities. There may be family circumstances in which you are greatly needed, but these are usually temporary, not a job for life.

Your top-priority task now is to build a worthwhile, new life for yourself, with your own interests and your own friends, some treats which are actually what you enjoy, plus reasonable care of your health. Your grandchild will be part, but only a part, of it. This is how it should be, and what better could you do for your family than to demonstrate to the two younger generations that middle age and onwards is nothing to dread but a time of opportunity, a positive experience of which you, for one, are making a success.

HEALTH

You don't need to be a hypochondriac but check that your current lifestyle is going to keep your body/mind machine in good running order. That means the right food, exercise and mental stimulus with sleep and rest as required.

What to Eat

Times have changed in our lifetime due to the mass of effort-saving technology. A favourite slimming diet of the 1890s recommended 2 lbs (900g) of steak and 2 lbs of cod, plus vegetables, washed down with 8 pints (4.5 litres) of hot water and some claret, every day. The intake recommended by government experts for the late 1990s for ordinary adults, not slimmers, comprises 5 servings of fruit or vegetables daily, plus 3 or 4 slices of wholemeal bread or other carbohydrate with a smidgen of low-fat spread, skimmed milk and 4 oz (115g) meat or other protein a day. For the precise amounts you need to monitor your weight, aiming to keep within 5 lbs (2.5 kg) either way of the norm. For a woman of 5ft 4ins (1.63 metres) a healthy weight is around 8 st 9 lbs (55 kg).

With a mixed diet on the lines suggested, you won't need extra vitamins but make sure – at our age – that you have enough iron and calcium:

- *Iron* can be found in liver, red meat, eggs, All-bran, dark treacle, plain chocolate.
- *Calcium* can be found in cheese, milk, yoghurt, sardines, white bread.

Your Weight

Don't let your weight creep up too far, so as to prevent strain on your heart and blood pressure, your joints and muscles. Nor should you let yourself become very underweight since this makes you more susceptible to infections and fractures.

Exercise

The watchword is regularity, for example, half-an-hour's brisk walk every day or 40 minutes three times a week as a minimum. Swimming, badminton, golf, croquet, tennis and table tennis are excellent at any age but jogging, squash and running a marathon are more strain than gain for the over-fifties. The object of exercise is to keep your muscles up to scratch, ward off osteoporosis and arthritis, boost your circulation all over, including to your brain – and hopefully to give you some enjoyment.

Sleep

You may be tired in the body, but you will have noticed that your brain does not want to go to sleep for nearly as long as in the past. Six hours is plenty for most people from sixty onwards. Don't aim for the impossible but learn to rest your muscles while keeping your mind occupied with sedentary evening pastimes: TV, radio, socializing, reading, listening to music and the crafts. If you have difficulty with sleeping, don't rush along to the doctor for a sleeping pill: they soon lose their efficacy and anyway tend to make you dopey in the day. Try keeping to a regular bedtime routine, with the room warmed up, a hot bath and a hot milky drink and a biscuit, and a radio by the bed, preferably with a sleep button. Don't go to bed at nursery time and don't lie in bed in the morning, after you have woken up – even if you had a bad night – and don't have a daytime nap. It's a matter of finding other things to do or think about when you no longer require so many hours' sleep.

MOT and Running Repairs

In spite of a healthy lifestyle, some parts of the body may begin to show signs of wear in the granny years. An occasional check-up, even if you feel well, can nip trouble in the bud. Diabetes, for example, frequently develops at fifty-plus, but it can be prevented from becoming a serious nuisance if it is detected by a urine or blood test before you have any definite symptoms. The same applies to most cancers.

Now is a good time to check out your hearing – are you losing some of the higher pitched consonants in conversation? It makes people sound as if they are mumbling. A hearing aid is like switching on the light, for your ears, and the modern ones are so tiny as to be virtually invisible. You are also likely to find reading glasses an added convenience now. HRT (hormone replacement therapy) may give your general health and mood a boost, and if you are well past the change, Kliofem is handy. You don't get a monthly bleed, but if you are in your sixties or seventies you may need to begin with a weekly or twice-weekly dose: discuss this with your GP or gynaecologist.

If some of the larger body parts are getting worn, help is at hand: new hips and new knees for old, refurbishment of the blood supply of the heart, new day-care operations for hernia. All these are available, free, if you need them, plus a range of drugs to suit every condition.

THE REAL YOU

All that is the physical side. The essential you is mental and emotional. While your body may need less nourishment, your mind is ready for more at this stage. Nourishment for your brain – the organ of mind – means new interests, new people with whom to exchange views, new things to do.

If you have a job that you've been doing for ages, you still need the refreshment of something different to think about. If you don't have an outside job at present, you might consider what is possible, either paid or in the voluntary sector. Perhaps you could do a course, learn a practical skill, join a local organization, take up bridge – to enrich your life. You will find that there are plenty of other people like you involved in all these activities. It is an opportunity to make new friends, something which can be difficult if you are over sixty.

None of this means missing out on being a granny, but you will be a better one if your mind is alert and well furnished with ideas, and your body as healthy as it can be.

Self-care and Appearance

This is important, not vanity. Looking good is a tonic for other people as well as for yourself. You are lucky with your complexion: no more oily or spotty skin but one that is fine and delicate, and looks its best with a minimum of make-up. Hair-colouring can be counter-productive because your naturally paler skin tone cannot stand up to the strong, artificial hair shades. Grey round the forehead and temples is becoming, even if the rest is darker.

Similarly, the softer shades and soft materials for your clothes will suit you better than raw, harsh reds and yellows. They don't have to be dreary in style – today anything is allowed, so long as you feel right in it.

Moisturizing creams and bath oils are kind to your skin – the baby preparations are ideal. Scented soaps and bubble baths are out (as they can provoke cystitis and thrush), but it is well worth wearing a fragrance. Small children, more than others, appreciate a granny who always brings the scent of flowers, sandalwood or something special. As a grandmother now myself, it still reminds me of my granny, my mother's mother, when I smell Rose Geranium.

You Are of Value

It is an achievement to be a grandmother: proof that you have successfully reared your own family. Even the law, via the Children Act, recognizes your worth to your grandchildren. Splendid, but there is more to you than being a useful appendage to the younger generations. Through the years while you have been gathering knowledge and experience, your personality has grown and developed.

This stage is like another adolescence: you have learned and matured and now you are able to handle more freedom of choice in the way you organize your life. You are no longer tied to the school run for as far ahead as you could envisage, although you may still take a turn. You haven't got to find a baby-sitter when you want to go out – although you may do some baby-sitting yourself on occasion. If you are working, at least you haven't got to learn the ropes from the beginning. All this adds up to freedom and more time.

The future may seem strange, uncharted territory, and there is a temptation to latch on to what you know – your children and grandchildren. Of course they fill an important place in your heart, but your top responsibility, now, is to yourself. Be kind to yourself – and your partner. Fit in now some of the things you had always wanted to do, if only you'd had the time. It does not have to be dramatic and costly, like a six-months' safari in Africa, but an afternoon in an art gallery, a day or week at a health farm, trying your hand at water-colours, making a herb garden – or a patch-work cushion – writing a book, or renewing contact with friends from the past. What is on your list?

Always plan to have a treat to look forward to: again it doesn't have to be big or complicated, so long as you like it, or think you might.

If you can play the granny role as required and cope with your own life and its problems happily too, you will reap a harvest of love and appreciation across the generations, to last you all the years of your life. At the crunch there will always be willing and loving help, but don't let it be too often or too long-term.

Your Turn Summary

- Reactions to retirement
- Six pitfalls
- Looking after your health
- What to expect at sixty-plus
- Food for your health
- Looking good

Appendix 1
Toys and Play

GIVING A TOY to your grandchild is the delightful essence of being a grandparent. It is a gift of love and enjoyment – and education, too – in the one package. It will be a frequently used, happy reminder of you – if you choose it well. That's the problem. If you'd gone to William Hamley's pioneer toyshop in London in 1760 you'd have found the top lines were rag dolls, wooden animals, especially horses, tin soldiers and hoops – and not much else. Making a choice would not have been too difficult. For example, there were no soft, cuddly toys until the 1880s – Teddy didn't come on the scene until 1902. There were no model railways until 1921, let alone radio-controlled cars and computer games.

Nowadays you need a guide book to find your way round the crowded, colourful shelves and to do some advance planning as well. Toys are so important to a child's development and sometimes so expensive that it is worth taking trouble over the selection. This applies whether your grandchild is with you, or you are on your own. Play is essential practice for living, the child's equivalent of work. Toys are the tools. See the solemn concentration on a two-year-old's face when she is putting her dolly to bed – with suitable admonitions; or when a young engineer of six is constructing a crane that works.

Playthings give pleasure and provide training in both physical and mental skills, from a bouncy rubber ball to a toy typewriter. there is a particular satisfaction in making the toy yourself, and there is a section about it later in the chapter. But there are lots of toys we can't make, for instance the ball or the typewriter, while modern technology can work wonders for us. Besides, the pace of modern life leaves us with so little time, more especially for us women.

POINTS TO REMEMBER WHEN YOU ARE BUYING A TOY

Safety is paramount, so look out for:

- sharp points and edges
- loose small parts, or toys that you assemble from small pieces – unless your grandchild is three-and-a-half or more. Younger than that, children tend to test everything by putting it in their mouths
- check soft toys for weak seams and stuffing coming out, and insecurely fixed eyes, especially glass ones on wires. Go for firmly attached plastic or cloth eyes
- doll's hair coming out
- strings and ties longer than 12 ins (30 cm)
- batteries that a young child could get at
- toys for tinies that look like food or sweets
- insubstantial, unstable or rickety sit-and-ride or climbing toys

Look for the Lion Mark which shows that the toy meets the British Safety Standards, or CE, referring to European Safety Standards.

Other points:

- do consider your grandchild's age and don't be afraid of getting something too babyish: we all tend to see our own grandchildren as phenomenally advanced
- beware of the toy that is all the rage this Christmas. The price is bound to be artificially hyped up but the fashion won't last. These toys are usually greeted with delight and found disappointing – besides, the parents have usually been pressurized into buying it already
- if in doubt, go for simple toys: there's less to go wrong and more scope for imagination
- don't choose what appeals to your adult taste, for

instance natural wood and a design award. Children like clear, basic colours

- check that the car-track, railway or climbing frame will fit comfortably into the child's bedroom or playroom. If not it will be a constant source of conflict or never used.
- similarly, if the toy takes time and a grown-up to set it up it will tend to stay in its box
- give just one present at a time, however big and generous your heart. It detracts from the joy of unwrapping it, inspecting it and trying it if the toy is one of a bunch. Some seven-year-olds demand lots of presents, not to enjoy but to boast about to their school-mates
- don't be seduced by size. A bear too big to carry isn't nearly as good a companion as one that your grandchild can take around everywhere, including to bed
- don't be dismayed if the first thing he or she does is to take the new toy apart. This is the flip side of constructive play
- don't feel a failure if, after a superficial inspection, your toy is apparently discarded. When the excitement of the birthday or Christmas has subsided your grandchild will come back to it
- remember some spare batteries, for a moving toy may be used non-stop, especially if it is a weekend or a holiday.
- will it run on the type of flooring that is available? Thick pile, fitted carpets are deadly to cars

Apart from pleasure, do you want the toy to help your grandchild in any particular way?

To stimulate the imagination:
- dolls, dolls' houses
- trucks, cars and garages
- nurse or policeman gear
- detective or naturalist set
- dressing-up clothes
- soldiers, guns, aeroplanes
- play house, tent

To practise co-ordination:
- stacking and posting toys
- coloured paper, paste and scissors
- screwdriver and nuts
- models to make

To encourage speech:
- toy telephone – preferably two
- glove or finger puppets
- tea set (big enough to drink from)

For discrimination:
- card games (snap, Lotto etc)
- jigsaws
- posting/sorting boxes

To strengthen muscles:
- trike, bike, rocking toys
- swing
- balls

For self-expression:
- pots of bright, wash-off paint
- clay, play-dough
- crayons, water colours
- toy xylophone, drum, recorder

Definitely educational:
- huge selection designed to help with telling the time, numbers, pre-reading, science, geography, history etc

AGE CHECK

You'd expect, as it is second time round for us, that we grannies would find it easy to judge which toys are suitable for different ages. But memory is deceptive and we are apt to remember our children best at the tiny-to-toddler stages and in adolescence. To make matters worse there is also an enormous individual variation in children's tastes and their rate of development. The lists below are meant as an approximate guide only. In general, children will go on enjoying toys which were suitable when they were a year younger, but may not get much pleasure in those aimed at older youngsters.

The First Year

First 6 months:
- an absolutely unbreakable rattle, not too heavy for a tiny hand to hold
- a tinkling, spring-hung mobile
- traditionally, the first gift from Granny to new baby is a small, soft, cuddly animal. It won't mean anything much to your grandchild to start with, but it isn't a silly present. Just by being around Baby in his cot or pram, it will develop into a companion that shares everything, and ultimately a lifelong friend. This is the toy that he, or more likely she, will take with her to college as a teenager

Sitting up:
- ball with a bell inside
- cloth-covered foam bricks to grab – and drop
- nesting and stacking toys
- sturdy little car with peg person that comes out
- pop-up or musical toys where you press a button
- roll-back toys and wobbly balls: you have to help Baby to play with these

One Year
Go for solidly made, simple shapes, bright colours.
- push-along toys
- toys to walk with: wagon or doll's pushchair/pram with handle to help balance
- interesting, big balls
- soft plastic or cloth dolls and animals
- bricks, used to load wagon

One-and-a-half

- pull-along toys, and more push-alongs
- domestic equipment: pots and pans, plastic hammer, dustpan and brush
- doll or animal: will now be carried around, so best of manageable size

Two Years

- bath toys
- doll's clothes and equipment
- screwdrivers and big screws: wooden
- posting box
- lorry or cart to take toys, Teddy around
- little cars
- play-dough, finger paints
- sand toys
- huge beads to thread
- basic trike with wide-spaced wheels

Three Years

- toys that move independently, battery or wind-up
- doll's house
- chunky wooden railway that fits together
- shop, garage, hospital
- household equipment

Four Years

Three-year list plus:
- construction toys with designs to follow
- simple jigsaws
- more realistic cars, trains, dolls

Five Years

Four-year list plus:
- play house or wigwam
- scooter, skipping rope
- scissors and magazines to cut out, paste

Six Years

Earlier lists plus:
- board games with dice
- dominoes and draughts
- nurse, policeman etc uniform: very good at make-believe at this age, and keen about all she/he does

Seven Years

- two-wheel bike
- soft ball and bat, for bat and ball games
- jigsaws
- model aeroplanes, trains and boats

Eight Years

- table games, not too simple; card games
- electronic cars, remote control
- Scalextric, electric train sets
- hand-held computer games

Nine-plus

- computer games
- Pictionary, Trivial Pursuit, Cluedo, Monopoly (still)
- Scrabble
- 'green' games, about saving the world
- chess, backgammon

From now on your grandchild will have his or her own very definite needs and tastes, which must be your guide. Any tools or sports equipment should now be miniature sizes of the real articles, not flimsy toys.

Best Sellers

Expensive: toys to ride, computer games, electronic cars
Other: dolls, cars, trains, construction toys, dressing-up sets, table games, jigsaws, soft toys.

DIY toys

You can't run up a computer game on the kitchen table, but for a grandchild up to the age of seven you can make toys that give just as much pleasure as the shop-bought. The cost is tiny and the recipient may derive some extra pleasure from helping in the manufacture. Children always enjoy actually doing something, especially if it is something a grown-up is engaged in. That's how they learn.

Don't feel embarrassed if your efforts don't come up to professional standard. Toys that are too perfect or too sophisticated – for instance a doll that cries and wets itself or a toy parrot that says three mechanical phrases – leave no scope for a child's imagination. Another plus point for the home-made is that most of these toys are expendable. It isn't a tragedy if they get broken, and when the novelty wears off they can be replaced by something different.

Junk Collection

If you go in for making toys you will suddenly find treasure in things you would have thrown away before. You'll look out for cardboard boxes of all shapes and sizes, plastic lids, old socks and tights, scraps of material, oddments of wool, plastic food containers, Christmas cards and magazines.

You should also lay in supplies of:

- self-hardening clay
- non-toxic paint
- glue, paste
- scissors, knife, needle and thread
- dowel rods
- card

Ideas that Have Worked for Other Grannies

Knitted doll or animal: Even if you are not into knitting, this is such a small amount that anyone can do it. Knit four narrow rectangles for the arms and legs and a longer, square one for the body. The head section needs to be rounded – at any rate when you sew it together. All the parts need sewing up and filling with plastic foam (washable), and the various parts then joined firmly together. A ribbon helps to define the neck. If it is an animal you need ears from tiny knitted pieces or felt. You sew the features in with wool, and for a doll the hair is also wool sewn into position, with a few free ends round the face. A doll needs a dress or skirt, a bear or rabbit nothing.

This type of soft toy will be easy for Baby to clutch and wave around and is completely harmless.

Cloth doll or animal: Cut out the size and shape you require twice. Sew both bits together right side inwards, leaving a gap to turn it inside out and fill with foam stuffing. Sew up the last bit and either paint on the face or sew the features in wool. The hair is wool, too, firmly sewn down. Clothes can be as simple or as elegant as you like: knitted ones are easy to take on and off.

Kite: A windy day toy. Start with two thin dowel rods, one two-thirds the length of the other, and fix them together with string, in a cross. Cut notches in the ends of the dowels, and stretch a thin string from notch to notch to make a frame. Cut out paper to fit the frame with an overlap all round and fix over the string with sticky tape. Make a tail with twists of coloured paper tied into a length of string. Finally, fix a string to each end of the long dowel and about two-thirds of the way up attach the string to fly it with.

Woolly ball toys: Cut out two cardboard discs 3–4 inches (8–10 cm) across with a central hole, like a Polo mint. Put the two rings together, and wind wool through the hole in the middle and round the edge, over and over, until it is quite tightly packed. Then cut between the two discs, slip a piece of nylon wool between them and tie tightly round the wool at the centre. Take the cardboard discs away – and hey presto! Trim any untidy ends.

With woolly balls of different sizes and colours you can make a tiny mobile to hang on Baby's pushchair/pram, or join them together to make various animals. 'Big' grandchildren of, say, four, enjoy making one woolly ball themselves.

Doll's house: You need four shoe-boxes, to glue or tape together to make four rooms: the open sides facing forwards. You can arrange a sloping roof with red-painted card, to go on top. The walls of the rooms can be papered with wrapping paper or sponge-painted, and stamps make good pictures. Windows or doors may be cut out with a sharp, pointed knife – but the fun and the magic come with the furnishings. Scraps of material make curtains, and a square of thicker fabric does for carpet. Match-boxes convert to chests of drawers and beds, cotton reels with lids fixed on top make tables. Conkers in season or half corks with pin legs and backs are good for chairs, while bits of eggboxes, padded, make a three-piece suite. It transforms everything when you paint it or use stick-on plastic – although it is fiddly, you will find that your imagination carries you from one inspiration to another.

Doll's house people: A baby is a sausage of pink fabric with a ribbon to divide body from head, and features sewn in, wrapped in a tiny shawl. The other dolls are made from pipe-cleaners. Twist two together to make the body, ending in the legs and feet, and use another to make the arms. Wind wool round and round the trunk and limbs to make them thicker, and the right colour. Sew on a head made from a small circle of stretchy cloth, with wool hair and features. Clothes come from small pieces of material – sometimes better put on before the head is finally fixed.

Theatre: This is simpler than a doll's house. You need one cardboard box, with the open side upwards. Cut an arch-shaped opening large enough for the audience to see the actors in the front and a slot to manipulate them through at each side. Paint the inside and outside of the box with theatrical decoration round the arch. Paint different backdrop scenery to fit the box, and attach at the top to a dowel rod long enough to hang on the top of the box. The characters may be cut-outs from a magazine or comic, or pipe-cleaner people. You move them by a rod or thread fixed to the top, or a rod or length of cardboard fixed to the bottom of the model and running horizontally, to manipulate through a side slot.

Clay toys: Unless you have a kiln, buy the self-hardening type. You can make beads by cutting a sausage of clay into suitable lengths, shaping them, then threading onto a knitting needle: paint when dry. Clay animals include mice, hedgehogs and snails, or cats and rabbits – sitting down. Paint them and use beads for eyes and noses, and card for ears. A clay Aladdin's lamp is something your helper will enjoy making. Small hands can fashion the clay into a little bowl, with one side stretched out to make an Aladdin shape. Putting a night-light in the middle and painting a weird, magic pattern on it when it is dry completes a satisfying project. Good to have on the table at a birthday party.

Clothes pegs dolls and soldiers: These need pipe cleaner arms, a skirt if they are female (elastic thread waist) and otherwise painted clothes and faces.

Puppets: Finger puppets are made from an old cloth glove, such as a cleaning type, with sewn features and hair, and extras like hats, ears, beards. Hand puppets – with one arm on the thumb side – are made by cutting out material from a template of your grandchild's hand – twice. Both pieces are sewn together – except where the hand goes in – then turned inside out and the face painted or sewn on, plus hair etc fixed on as the mood takes you.

Home-made board games: These are designed on the Snakes and Ladders principle, but using familiar places and situations and adding amusing penalties and rewards. The essentials are a sizeable piece of card for the base, or an old tray if you have one, and paint. It makes it more interesting if you stick a few 'landmarks' round the course – a twig tree, a stone for a rock, beads for jewels, a mysterious sign. All you need now is a dice.

Once you get the toy-making bug, you will find ideas crop up all the time. You can make a windmill, a baby's room mobile, a witch's outfit plus broom, various musical instruments, a mop-head doll. I especially like making a seascape:

You need a bowl or big dish half filled with water. Big stones with moss put on them make islands, and the boats are walnut shells with leaf or paper sails fixed in with a little knob of clay. This is more of a toy for me than my grandchild – since I can't wrap it up and give it to her. But isn't this a bonus of being a granny – the chance to play again – and to read again the books we love?

Appendix 2
Books and Stories

JUST AS a cuddly soft toy is a traditional gift from Granny to grandchild, long before the baby can appreciate it, so it is time-honoured practice for you to give your small grandchild a book that he won't understand at first. Like the cuddly bear, he will come to love and treasure it like an old friend, especially if it is one of the classics, from Beatrix Potter to Lewis Carroll.

Books are a magic carpet for the mind, transporting the reader into a faraway land of fantasy, or the complexities of molecular biology. Imagination is a uniquely human attribute, and the basis of creativity and inspiration. It is also necessary for such mundane activities as planning a picnic. Books and stories provide the nourishment for imagination, which in children is especially receptive. All children's play is an exercise in imagination: how else could a kitchen table with a rug over it turn into a house?

Learning to read is an essential skill for living, but it can become a chore at school: enough to put a child off books for life. As a granny, you can help them to be a source of pleasure. Children of equal intelligence vary widely in the age at which their brains are ready to read. Among the slow readers who made good are Louis Pasteur, William Thackeray, George Bernard Shaw and Henry Ford. On average, children grasp the rudiments at about seven.

Up to fifteen months, your grandchild is in the pre-book phase, but she is busy learning to talk. She – or he – will enjoy hearing over and over such action rhymes as Pat-a-cake, Ride a Cock Horse and Pussycat, Pussycat. Soon she will enjoy hearing the same story again and again, word for word. It is a tiny step to connect the words with pictures in a book.

Baby books

These are basically picture books.

Bath Books

These are made of impervious plastic and they float: the Rev. Awdry's trains feature in one of them. In general, it doesn't seem sensible to use a book as a bath toy since other books and water are not compatible.

Cloth

Baby can clutch a wide range of these, but they are not like real books.

Board and Plastic Card

These are best. Favourites are:

- Mick Inkpen: *Wibbly Pig* series
- Judith Kerr: *Mog's Kittens* series

Classics to Keep

These are suitable to give at any age up to six:

- Beatrix Potter series (separate or complete)
- *National Trust Book of Nursery Rhymes*
- A A Milne's stories and poems (separate or complete)
- Alison Uttley's *Little Grey Rabbit* series (separate or complete)

To help your grandchild enjoy and value books they should be associated with love, and warmth and comfort: in a snug situation on your knee.

What You Can Expect

Fifteen months: She'll grab the book, pat the pictures and 'help' to turn the pages.

Eighteen months: He'll show a genuine interest in the pictures and enjoy pointing to – say – a dog or a baby if you ask him to. He'll turn two or three pages together.

Two years: She'll say the names of the animals, car etc pictured, and now turn the pages singly. She may pretend to pick up an object from the picture: this is a fine joke. She links the pictures with the story and wants to hear an exact repetition of the words each time. She'll disapprove if you try to skip a page here and there.

Three to four to five years: Real stories in which something happens come into their own. To give your grandchild the delight of demonstrating how clever he is, let him finish some of the well-rehearsed sentences in the story, and later on ask, 'What do you think happens next?'

BOOKS FOR UNDER-FOURS

These are among the most popular with tinies and their adults:

- Janet and Allan Ahlberg: *The Baby's Catalogue*
                                   Peepo
                                   Each Peach Pear Plum
- Eric Hill: *Spot* series, big choice and wonderful illustrations
- Eric Carle: *The Very Hungry Caterpillar* – a best-seller for more than twenty years
- Jan Pienkowski: *Meg and Mog* series
- Virginia Miller: *Eat Your Dinner*
- Sarah Hayes: *This is the Bear*
- Jez Alborough: *It's the Bear* – hardback, and more expensive than the others
- Sara McBratney: *Guess How Much I Love You* – also hardback
- David McKee: *Elmer*: the famous patchwork Elephant
- Babette Cole: *Dr Dog* – hardback

Hardbacks are around £8.99, others mainly £3.99.

FOUR TO SIX YEARS

- Janet and Allan Ahlberg: *Starting School*
- Roald Dahl: *Minpins, Enormous Crocodile* – Dahl is the most popular all-round children's author
- Jill Murphy: *All in One Piece*
- Judith Kerr: *Mog the Forgetful Cat*

- Roger Hargreaves: *Mr Men* and *Little Miss* series (only £1.25 each)

Old Favourites, as Much Loved as Ever

- Michael Bond: *Paddington Bear* series
- John Cunliffe: *Postman Pat* series
- Reverend Awdry: *Thomas the Tank Engine* series
- De Brunhoff: *Babar*
- Katherine Hale: *Orlando* series
- Maurice Sendak: *Where the Wild Things Are* – delightful
- and the classics mentioned above: Potter, Milne and Uttley: at this age your grandchild can enjoy them thoroughly.

SIX TO EIGHT YEARS

- Tony Bradman: *Dilly the Dinosaur* – excellent, modern series
- Henrietta Brandford: *Dimanche Diller* – this book won an award and is only £2.99
- Joyce Brisley: *Milly Molly Mandy* – everlasting favourite
- Jeff Brown: *Flat Stanley*
- Humphrey Carpenter: *Mr Majeika*
- Helen Cresswell: *Meet Posy Bates*
- Pat Hutchins: *The House That Sailed Away*
- Dorothy Edwards: *My Naughty Little Sister* – another immortal
- Ann Jungman: *Vlad the Drac* – good new series
- Jill Murphy: *The Worst Witch* – brilliant, funny
- Dick King-Smith: *The Hodgeheg* – very popular author, who has written many books
- Jill Tomlinson: *The Owl Who Was Afraid of the Dark*
- Margery Williams: *The Velveteen Rabbit*
- Ursula Moray Williams: *Gobbolino the Witch's Cat*

Although your grandchild will love you reading to her, she may also want to show you that she can read too.

EIGHT TO TWELVE YEARS

This is a wonderful age for reading – your grandchild can read for himself, and his imagination can fly solo.

Contemporary Authors

- Roald Dahl: *The BFG, Charlie and the Chocolate Factory, Boy* – and others: everything by this author is enjoyed.
- L Fitzhugh: *Harriet the Spy*
- Philip Ridley: *Meteorite Spoon*
- Sylvia Waugh: *Mennyms* and *Mennyms in the Wilderness* – a prize-winning book
- Hilary McKay: *Exiles* and *Exiles at Home* – another prize-winning author
- Anne Fine: *Goggle Eyes, Flour Babies* – prize-winner and popular with the children as well as the grown-ups
- Paul Jennings: *Unbearable* – popular playground author, right in fashion
- Gillian Cross: *The Great Elephant Chase*
- Brian Jaques: *Redwall* series – junior school favourite
- Russell Stannard: *The Time and Space of Uncle Albert*
- Alan Garner: *Elidor*
- Robert Westall: *Machine Gunners*
- E B White: *Charlotte's Web*
- Michael Foreman: *War Game*
- *Kingfisher* series of treasuries of short stories by famous contemporary writers, for example, *Funny Stories, Animal Stories, Bedtime Stories* etc

Earlier and Classic Authors

- Laura Ingalls Wilder: *The Little House on the Prairie* – series
- Lynne Reid Banks: *The Indian in the Cupboard*
- Louisa M Alcott: *Little Women, Good Wives*
- Enid Blyton: *Famous Five* and other series – all still popular; easy to read and give children confidence in their reading.
- Carolyn Keene: *Nancy Drew* series – mysteries solved by young detective

- Franklin Dixon: *The Hardy Boys* – also popular mystery stories
- Willard Price: *Amazon Adventure* – and many others
- Mary Norton: *The Borrowers*
- Joan Aiken: *The Wolves of Willoughby Chase* – and numerous others
- Helen Cresswell: *Moondial* and *Bagthorpes* series
- Rudyard Kipling: *Just So Stories*
- Jack London: *White Fang*
- C S Lewis: *Chronicles of Narnia*
- Michelle Margorian: *Goodnight Mr Tom*
- E Nesbit: *The Railway Children* – and others
- Philippa Pierce: *Tom's Midnight Garden*
- Arthur Ransome: *Swallows and Amazons* – and others
- Ian Serralier: *The Silver Sword*
- Noel Streatfield: *Ballet Shoes*
- Rosemary Sutcliffe: *Eagle of the Ninth*
- Mark Twain: *The Adventures of Tom Sawyer*

Twelve and over

- Judy Blume: *Superfudge*
  Deenie – top favourite American author
- Paula Danzinger: *Earth to Matthew* – favourite English author
- Berlie Doherty: *Dear Nobody* – prize-winner
- S E Hinton: *The Outsiders*
- Robert Leeson: *Coming Home*
- Robert O'Brien: *Z for Zachariah*
- Robert Swindells: *Stone Cold* – won a medal, also *Brother in the Land*
- Sue Townsend: *The Secret Diary of Adrian Mole Aged 13¾*
- Cynthia Voigt: *On Fortune's Wheel*
- Robert Westall: *Urn Burial*
- Chris Westwood: *Brother of Mine*
- Paul Zindel: *Pigman*
- Lois Duncan: *Don't Look Behind You*

- Margaret Mahy: *Memory*
- Mildred T Taylor: *Roll of Thunder Hear My Cry*

Most of today's teenagers are keen on the *Point* series published by Scolastic: there is a large range with series called *Point Crime, Point Romance, Point Scifi*, and the most popular of all – *Point Horror*. New ones come out all the time. They may not be wonderful from the literary aspect, but they do keep up the teenager's interest in reading – important in this TV age.

GIFT BOOKS – TO LOOK AFTER AND KEEP
The selection for the very young is on p. 162.

- *Walker Book of Fairy Tales*
- *Walker Book of Poetry*
- Hans Christian Anderson: *Stories* and *Fairy Tales*
- Morpurgo: *Arthur: High King of Britain*
- Perham: *King Arthur and the Legends of Camelot*
- Lewis Carroll: *Alice in Wonderland, Alice Through the Looking Glass* – gift set
- J M Barrie: *Peter Pan*
- C S Lewis: complete set of his children's works: £50 hardback, £28 paperback
- *Hutchinson Treasury of Children's Literature*

READ ME A STORY
Even we sophisticated adults enjoy hearing someone reading or telling us a story. Radio 4's 'Book at Bedtime' sounds juvenile, but it is for us; and there is the afternoon story – for grown-ups too. Children love you to read to them, although at about eight their dignity suggests that they can do it for themselves (except when they are ill). There is an in-between stage when your grandchild wants to read to you. This requires tact and patience from you.

Patience is needed to allow for the slow pace, and tact in helping occasionally and discreetly with a difficult word. Of course you must be generous with your praise, for reading practice is something so important that you want to reward it.

Sometimes you haven't a book at hand – for instance if the car has broken down and you have to wait for the AA, or you are on a walk – and telling a story is a delightful way to keep your grandchild happy. I often tell my grandson a story while I am doing the ironing, if I am looking after him for few hours.

Fairy tales are the easiest to remember and they deal in a wonderful way with the fundamental human emotions: love, jealousy, greed and kindness. Another plus point is that in the end, after a brave struggle, the good people aways come out on top. Unlike reading a story to a small-sizer, when you are actually telling it, you don't have to get every word precisely right. And you can alter the story or the names of the characters to suit your listener. You can give your repertoire a boost by reading – or re-reading – *Old Peter's Russian Tales*, by Arthur Ransome.

If you have several grandchildren, or you are especially interested in giving them the right books, you might think it worthwhile to subscribe to:

Books for Your Children: A Guide for Parents (3 issues a year)
FREEPOST BM 575, Birmingham B4 6BR.

Appendix 3
Milestones

THIS IS a route plan made up of averages. No child OUGHT to follow it exactly, and some will be younger, some older when they reach any particular point. What matters is to see where the youngster is on the long journey of childhood, so that you know what to look out for next. (Little Emma, pp. 32–7, went at her own, individual pace which was right for her.)

Brand New
- **Weight:** 5½–7½ lbs (2.5–4.3 kg)
- **Length:** 18–21 ins (46–53 cm)
        (Asian babies are not so big and heavy)
- Cries, with no tears
- Coughs, sneezes, yawns and sucks
- Likes a sweet taste (like human milk)

One Month
- Lifts head momentarily, lying on his/her tummy
- Little fists closed, thumb inside
- Grips your finger tightly, if you put it in his hand

Six Weeks
- Recognizes parents: smiles for real
- Coos, gurgles, 'ooo'
- Startled by loud noise
- Soothed by mother's voice
- Turns head and eyes to listen and watch
- Copies putting tongue nearly out

Twelve Weeks

- Can lift head and upper chest – for photograph
- Fun with hands: looks at them while he opens and closes them
- Makes a sweep towards things he wants
- Babbles and laughs
- Doesn't like you to go away

Twenty Weeks

- Smiles at mirror when she sees herself
- Looks for toy she has dropped
- Makes sounds like ma, da, ka, ba and lll
- Can hold bottle of juice or milk

Six Months

- Excited when he sees you, friendly to everyone
- Lifts her head up, in readiness to be picked up
- Likes being bounced up and down, feet on your lap
- Likes playing Peep-bo
- Tests everything, including his toes, with his mouth
- 'Says' mama, dada, nana, baba
- Two middle bottom teeth may come through any time now: dribbles

One Year

- Sits up by herself, crawls
- Pulls herself onto her feet: staggers along if you hold a hand
- Drinks from a cup, with some help
- Understands such words as dog, teddy, Daddy
- Points with first finger for what he wants
- Shy of strangers (used not to be)

Eighteen Months

- Walks with feet a little apart, runs unsteadily
- Feeds herself with a spoon, manages cup alone
- Knows between six and twenty words, including parts of the body

- Can balance three or four blocks in a tower
- Likes looking at a book, on your knee, for a few minutes
- Plays by himself, but near you

Two Years
- Kicks a ball
- Goes up and down stairs, two feet per step, holding on
- Holds pencil in fist and does a round-and-round scribble
- Can balance six to seven bricks on top of each other
- Make-believe games, for instance making tea
- Likes to play near, but not necessarily with, other children
- Can take shoes and socks off and get them on
- Often says 'Mine', sentences of two or three words
- Tantrums maybe, when frustrated

Three Years
- Alternate feet going up stairs, coming down more difficult
- Rides a trike well
- Makes a train or a castle of up to nine blocks
- Threads big beads on a bootlace
- Games of 'let's pretend' with other children
- Eats with spoon and fork
- Holds pencil properly, can copy a circle and a cross
- Holds a conversation with you
- Dry at night – but may not be

Four Years
- Knows times of day and can look forward to things
- Understands if you have to go away temporarily
- Tells stories that he knows, and jokes: chatterbox
- May have difficulty pronouncing s, f, th or r still
- Can dress herself and use a knife at meals

Five Years
- Plays ball games, not very well
- Likes dressing up, drawing and painting

- Enjoys showing off what he or she can do, such as hopping, skipping, sliding, dancing to music
- Counts up to twenty, maybe more
- Knows nursery rhymes
- Puts features into faces, windows and doors in houses

Six Years

- Likes to climb – frame, trees
- Confident, a bit cheeky
- Learns easily: may get overloaded with home and school
- Beginning to read, needs help and practice
- Tooth fairy needed soon: front teeth getting wobbly

Seven Years

- More colds and sore throats than earlier
- Lots to do, interested in everything, busy
- Believes parents, teachers and you are strong, good and clever: make the most of this stage, it doesn't last
- Reads comics by himself
- Can write, with big uneven letters

Eight Years

- Keen on having money to buy, for instance, sweets
- Plays with a group of the same sex, for preference
- Can help with washing up, making a bed, cooking
- Generally truthful

Nine Years

- Little girls may have small breast buds
- Less childish; not so interested in fairy tales
- May have 'tummy aches' and leg pains under stress
- May be cheeky in a group and sulk about helping
- Good at making things and mending them
- Enjoys trips to museums and other grown-up outings
- Boys in a gang may exclude girls

Ten Years

- You can appeal to his or her reason, and explain why some things are not allowed
- Sense of fairness
- Loves secrets and mysteries
- Loyalty and hero-worship develop
- Talents, for instance for music, art begin to show
- Can read for interest and information

Eleven to Thirteen Years

- Growth spurt due to hormones, girls ahead of boys; periods
- Team games and competitive events: peak involvement
- Period of intense learning: academic types show up – education may take over too much
- Less going around in gangs, more friendships
- Rebellion against parents in particular: girls of thirteen often difficult with their mothers. Grandparents are OK
- Respond well to responsibility, not to being told
- Moody, thinking about religion, green issues, meaning of life

Fourteen Years

- Well into puberty: adulthood on the horizon
- Fluctuation between being an adult and a child: confused
- Likes to be treated as a near-adult
- Boys are noticeably stronger
- Girls are increasingly conscious of appearance, clothes
- Crushes on those of either sex, usually their own
- Sees parents as 'hopeless' and embarrassing
- Girls may get premenstrual tension
- Bedtime 9.30–10 pm

Fifteen Years

- Need for privacy and being alone: secretive
- May talk so quietly that you cannot catch it

- No longer wants to join in family outings, holidays
- Very keen on school *or* absolutely fed up with it
- Spare time and interest taken up with opposite sex
- Boys may get first hint of beard; acne

Sixteen Years

- Company of friends is top pleasure
- Mind on the future
- Understand value of money, interested in Saturday jobs
- Anxiety about examinations
- Boys keen on sport
- Boys may shave once a week: gooseberry look
- Girlfriends and boyfriends become important

Useful Addresses

UNITED KINGDOM

Grandparents' Federation
78 Cook's Spinney, Harlow, Essex CM20 3BL
01279 444964
(particularly helpful with grandchildren in care)

National Association of Grandparents
8 Kirkley Drive, Ashington, Northumbria NE63 9RD
01670 817036
(chatline for members on Sundays; conciliation and support with
family problems)

Family Rights Group
The Print House, 18 Ashwin Street, London E8 3DL
0171 923 2628
(legal advice and support network for grandparents of children in
local authority care)

Children Need Grandparents
2 Surrey Way, Laindon West, Basildon, Essex SS15 6PS
01268 414607
(advice and help to grandparents refused access)

The National Family Trust
101 Queen Victoria Street, London EC8 3DL
01242 227187

Stepfamily
72 Willesden Lane, London NW6 7TA
0171 372 0844
Counselling number: 0171 372 0846

UNITED STATES OF AMERICA
Foundation for Grandparenting
Box 326, Cohasset, MA 02025

Grandparents Anonymous
1924 Beverley, Sylvan Lake, MI 48320

Grandparents/Children's Rights
5728 Bayonne Avenue, Haslett, MI 48840

Grandparents Raising Grandchildren
P.O. Box 104, Colleyville, TX 76034

Grandparents Rights Organization
555 S. Woodward Avenue, Suite 600, Birmingham, MI 48009

National Association for Foster Grandparents Program
7500 Silver Star Road, Orlando, FL 32818

Foster Grandparents Program
1100 Vermont Avenue NW, 6th Floor, Washington, D.C. 20525

National Federation of Grandmother Clubs of America
203 N. Wabush Avenue, Suite 702, Chicago, IL 60601
(sponsors Grandmothers' Day: October – 2nd Sunday)

AUSTRALIA
Tresilian Family Care Centres
2 Shaw Street, Petersham, NSW 2049
02 569 8146

Older Women's Network
Local groups via telephone directory

Questionnaire

You can't set an exam paper in grannying. What's right and what's wrong, what may be true or otherwise, varies with the individuals and the circumstances. So in this questionnaire you are provided with four answers in each part, for you to put in your order of preference. The most common order in each case is given on pp. 179–80, so that you can check how near you come to the average. But there is nothing cut and dried: the object is to give you some interesting problems which may be relevant for you at some time.

1. Grannies are often accused of spoiling. You love seeing your little granddaughter enjoying herself, but your daughter-in-law thinks that sweets and ices are bad for the child. What should you do?
    a. Give the little one a treat when she is out with you, telling her to keep it secret.
    b. Uphold your daughter-in-law's views, pointing out that it shows that she cares, and find something other than food to give your grandchild pleasure.
    c. Reason with your daughter-in-law privately, saying that you think she may be too strict.
    d. Say in front of everyone: 'Do let me get her a choc-ice, like the other children'.

2. In discussing which school your grandchild should go to, you put a stress on:
    a. The size of the school and the class size.
    b. The one his father or grandfather went to.
    c. A happy atmosphere.
    d. The school's examination record.

3. You suspect that your grandchild feels insecure but is afraid to say so, if:
   a. She keeps getting colds.
   b. He has frequent tummy aches.
   c. She has begun stealing from her mother.
   d. His eczema has got worse.

4. When your grandchild asks you about death you should:
   a. Reassure him that only old people die.
   b. Tell her it is just like going to sleep.
   c. Tell him about Heaven although you don't believe in it.
   d. Let her go with the family to a funeral if she is five or more.

5. After the divorce your daughter-in-law refuses to let you see your grandchild. What should you do?
   a. Wait outside your granddaughter's school to snatch a few words with her when she comes out.
   b. Send little presents to your grandchild.
   c. Go on trying for months or years to win your daughter-in-law over, expecting it to take time for her to get over the hurt of the divorce.
   d. Apply to the courts for a contact order.

6. A good present for a fifteen-month-old is:
   a. A pull-along toy.
   b. A dolly's tea set.
   c. A big ball.
   d. A cart with a handle to push.

7. When you hear the news that a grandchild is on the way, regardless of the situation, you should:
   a. Ask if they are hoping for a boy or a girl.
   b. Say it's the best news since the end of the Cold War.
   c. Mention the dangers of smoking.
   d. Lay in a supply of plain biscuits to combat early pregnancy nausea.

8. Which granny stereotype do you resemble – a little?
   a. Efficient and dutiful.
   b. Live for your grandchild.
   c. Generous materially.
   d. Busy but supportive.

9. In giving personal presents to your grandchildren you weigh up:
   a. The parents' financial situation.
   b. Whether the grandchildren are ready-made or natural.
   c. How well they have behaved.
   d. None of these.

10. To be a good grandmother you must:
    a. Live nearby.
    b. Love your child first, your grandchild second.
    c. Keep up standards.
    d. Dump any other commitments at the drop of a hat.

11. You find the broken pieces of a favourite vase behind the sofa. Your grandson, aged nine, says he didn't do it. Your response is:
    a. You accept what he says and clear up the bits.
    b. You are plain furious.
    c. You say: 'What you mean is you wish you hadn't broken it. I expect it was an accident.'
    d. You tell him that it is wrong to tell lies.

12. Your top responsibility is:
    a. The welfare of the family.
    b. Your grandchild's happiness.
    c. Your own health and happiness.
    d. Your grandchild's grandfather.

Most Common Answers
1. b,c,d,a
2. c,d,b,a
3. b,c,d,a

4. d,a,c,b
5. c,b,d,a
6. d,c,a,b
7. b,d,c,a
8. d,a,b,c
9. d,a,c,b
10. b,c,d,a
11. c,a,b,d
12. c,d,a,b

Index